L. M. MONTGOMERY'S

❧

PRINCE EDWARD ISLAND

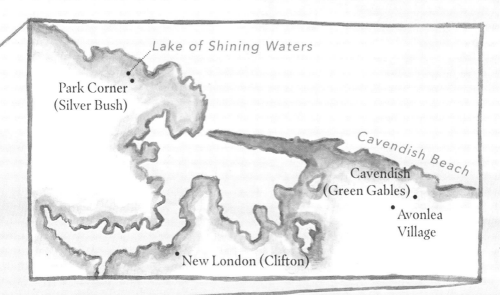

Lake of Shining Waters

Park Corner
(Silver Bush)

Cavendish Beach

Cavendish
(Green Gables)

Avonlea
Village

New London (Clifton)

Charlottetown

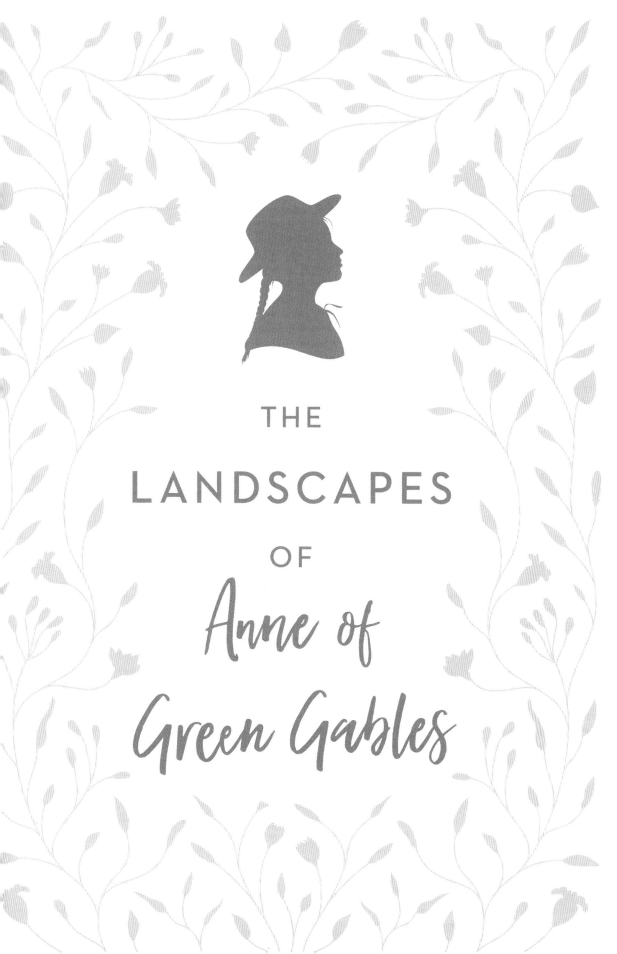

THE
LANDSCAPES
OF
Anne of
Green Gables

THE
LANDSCAPES
OF
Anne of
Green Gables

The Enchanting Island that
Inspired L. M. Montgomery

CATHERINE REID

Timber Press · Portland, Oregon

Page 2: Wheat ready for harvest.

Published in 2018 by Timber Press, Inc.

The Haseltine Building

133 S.W. Second Avenue, Suite 450

Portland, Oregon 97204-3527

timberpress.com

Printed in China

Text design by Hillary Caudle

Jacket design by Emily Weigel

ISBN-13: 978-1-60469-789-6

A catalog record for this book is available from the Library of Congress and the British Library.

CONTENTS

The good stars met in your horoscope,
Made you of spirit and fire and dew.

—ROBERT BROWNING, 1855

"**O**ld Prince Edward Island" is a good place in which to be born—a good place in which to spend a childhood. I can think of none better.

—THE ALPINE PATH

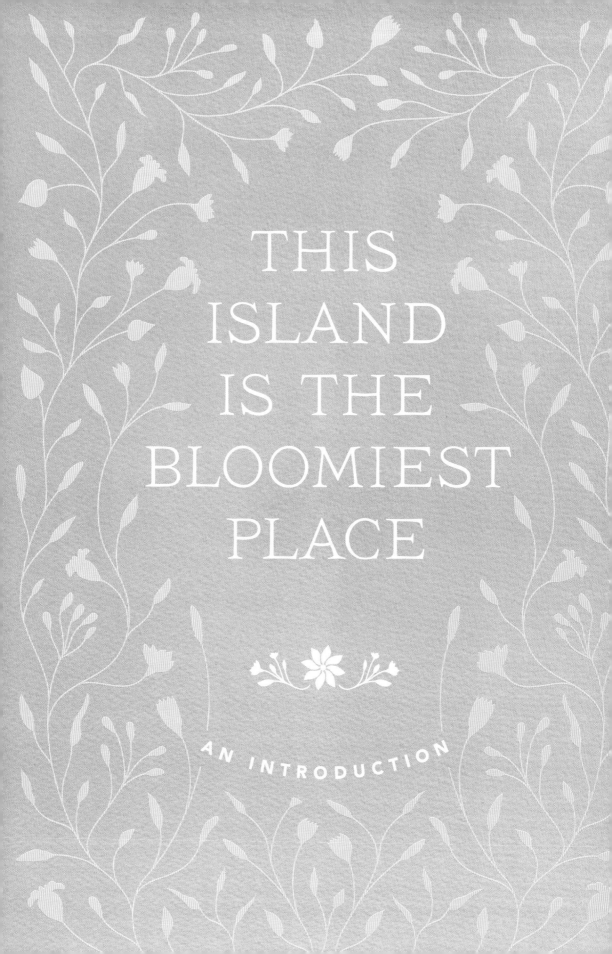

THIS ISLAND IS THE BLOOMIEST PLACE

AN INTRODUCTION

uring the course of her life, Lucy Maud Montgomery published twenty novels, more than five hundred short stories, hundreds of poems, and numerous essays. But it was her first and remarkable novel, *Anne of Green Gables* (1908), that garnered her a worldwide audience. The enthusiastic response to the book spurred an immediate request for more stories about the spunky, irrepressible Anne (an additional seven novels and three story collections fill out the rest of Anne's life), while *Anne of Green Gables* went through initial print runs at speeds that surprised author and publisher alike. In the subsequent century, the novel has sold over fifty million copies, been translated into twenty different languages, and spun off numerous films, plays, musicals, and television series.

Such popularity derives from the book's equally compelling features: the appeal of its storyline—elderly siblings want a boy from an orphanage to help them with farm work and are sent an odd scrawny girl instead—and the sheer force of Anne's personality, so garrulous, smart, and endearing that she quickly wins over Matthew and Marilla Cuthbert along with a wide array of island characters. Anne's imagination carries the book, as she manages to find the beauty in the bleak and the lesson in every disaster, beginning with the grim possibility of being returned to the orphanage.

Due to the phenomenal success of *Anne of Green Gables*, tourism is Prince Edward Island's second most important industry, with agriculture (number one) and fishing (number three) still as important as they were when Montgomery lived there. For the fan seeking the landscapes of Anne's old haunts, however, the level of new development can be startling; this is not the Prince Edward Island of the late 1890s, when Anne was gathering mayflowers by the armfuls and wandering fern-lined paths through the woods. One has to look beyond the modern conveyances to see the evidence of undisturbed woodlands, acres of farmland, and expanse of ocean just beyond, or squint in a way that blurs the adjacent golf course and amusement park, the buses and B&Bs, the tour groups and Anne look-alikes in their aprons and wigs with red braids. It is then that it becomes possible to see and sense all that a child—or the child in all of us—might have been able to learn and pursue in

12

"'MATTHEW CUTHBERT, WHO'S THAT?' SHE EJACULATED."

"Matthew Cuthbert," says the astonished Marilla, "who's that?"
Illustration by M. A. and W. A. J. Claus, from the 1908 edition.

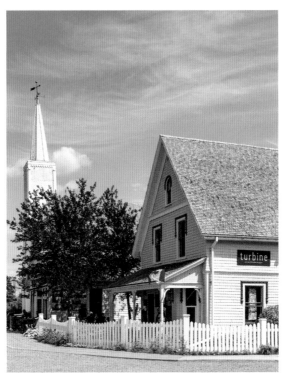

A street in Avonlea Village, which features original buildings from Montgomery's time as well as replicas of other period buildings; Montgomery modeled the fictitious Avonlea on the town of Cavendish, Prince Edward Island.

LEFT A road through the woods, looking much as it would have in Montgomery's day. In *Anne of Green Gables*, Montgomery referred to a similar lane as the Birch Path.

the Prince Edward Island of Anne's era. This book returns readers to the original landscape that so inspired one of literature's most memorable characters.

LUCY MAUD MONTGOMERY shares numerous similarities with the unforgettable Anne Shirley. Anne's parents died when she was an infant; Maud's mother also died when she was not-quite two, and her father decamped to the other side of the continent a few months later. Both are subsequently raised by elderly people—Maud by her mother's grim and stiff parents, and Anne by

15

Queen Anne's lace (*Daucus carota*)

a pair of unmarried siblings. Both are gregarious, intelligent, high achievers, excelling at their schoolwork and ranking top in their classes. Both attend one-room schools and later teach in them. Both delight in being in the midst of social whirls—whether berrying, recital-planning, or sharing pranks with their classmates; both also pursue justice ferociously and are adept at maintaining an iciness against those they feel have wronged them.

Most notably, though, it's when landscape and the imagination merge that their shared sensibility becomes most evident. They use many of the same names for their favorite places (Lover's Lane, the Lake of Shining Waters, the Haunted Wood) and spend as much time as possible wandering favorite spots (when she and her friends were young, Montgomery writes in an 1892 journal entry, "we fairly lived in the woods"). The great expanses of sea and field act like canvases for their imaginations, the quiet island beauty nourishing their souls.

In the first eight years of Lucy Maud Montgomery's surviving journals, the period she subsequently describes in *Anne of Green Gables*, nothing is rendered as poetically as are the scenes of nature—not clothing or playmates or the interiors of houses, not pets or schoolrooms or suitors. It's when she turns her attention to the surrounding land that the reader can feel her changing gears to one that evokes far more passion. In that shift of her gaze to the outdoors, the ordinary falls away, and the following sentences soar with aesthetic power. The subtle hues in a sunset, the

17

A field of clover, a cover crop that farmers might rotate with wheat, hay, corn, or potatoes.

changing colors of autumn, the winter scenes from a horse-drawn sleigh—all reverberate with new meaning when seen through Maud Montgomery's or Anne Shirley's eyes.

This shift in voice when turning to the landscape is especially noticeable when either girl is feeling uncertain, badly treated, or homesick, as in Anne's first hours with the Cuthberts, not knowing whether they would let her stay at Green Gables, or when Montgomery spends an awkward teenage year in Saskatchewan with her father and his new wife and realizes she has little place in their life there. To rally herself, each girl turns toward the natural world—looking out a window, walking down a wooded lane, or recovering a memory of some happy time spent outside—and almost immediately, as though a switch had been flipped, the prose vibrates with a new energy and the sorrow fades away.

18

Daisies, Queen Anne's lace, and goldenrod against a
yellow field of canola.

Maud Montgomery's beloved cousin and kindred spirit,
Frede Campbell, at Park Corner, in the splendor of
summer birches. Photo colorized by Maud Montgomery
in the 1920s.

In addition to documenting her life in her journals, Maud Montgomery, as she preferred to be called (islanders refer to her as "Lucy Maud"), also took photographs and created scrapbooks, which have helped later generations see and appreciate her world. Many of those photographs are included here, including some she colorized in the 1920s, along with images from some of the scrapbooks. Additional photographs by Kerry Michaels and Nick Jay provide contemporary context and atmosphere, and highlight the unique beauty that Prince Edward Island has retained over the years. The island's role in fueling the creativity that animates *Anne of Green Gables* continues to inspire those who come to witness it today, a landscape made to wander in and wonder about, with all the charm, as Maud Montgomery writes in *The Alpine Path*, of "the rich red of the winding roads, the brilliant emerald of the uplands and meadows, the glowing sapphire of the encircling sea."

I would like to go away on Sunday morning to the heart of some great solemn wood.

—THE SELECTED JOURNALS OF
L. M. MONTGOMERY, VOL. 1

KINDRED ORPHANS

THE LIVES OF

MAUD MONTGOMERY

AND

ANNE SHIRLEY

When Lucy Maud Montgomery created Anne Shirley, she contributed a memorable character to the rich literature of orphans: Jane Eyre, Tom Sawyer, and Huck Finn, along with Dickens's Oliver Twist, David Copperfield, and Pip of *Great Expectations*. Each of these children is tested again and again by cruel adults and brutal circumstances, yet each manages to triumph over adversity, and see and shape a kinder world along the way. Anne Shirley's situation follows a similar storyline—a young girl without family or friends, bounced from one bad situation to another, and then sent, unwanted, to a grim and crowded orphanage. By an odd stroke of luck, she finds herself en route to Avonlea, on Prince Edward Island, in response to Marilla and Matthew Cuthbert's request for a child to help with the work of their farm. Though not the boy the brother and sister had expected, once there, Anne proves

Prince Edward Island wheat fields, spruces, and fir trees. "There is no spot on earth more lovely," Montgomery wrote of the island, on December 11, 1890.

wildly successful at winning over her detractors and does so in a way that sets her apart from the other literary orphans. While the English moors, the Mississippi River, and the London underbelly are integral to their respective novels, Anne's relationship with the land of Prince Edward Island soon proves to be a critical source of inner strength.

As in the novels that preceded it, the strong draw of Anne's story is due as much to the orphan's charisma as to the setting where it takes place—in her case, the wooded paths, the orchards in bloom, the fields stretching out toward the sea. But the lasting gift of *Anne of Green Gables* is how the landscape also fuels Anne's prodigious imagination; it's where she goes when she needs sustenance; it's the example she'll hold onto for what is beautiful, what is possible. Anne's creator, Maud Montgomery, makes this abundantly clear in the ways she writes about the natural world. In

26

such passages, her writing soars, every sentence imbued with the kind of sensory detail that could only be rendered by someone who knew the scenes intimately and loved all she found there. In giving Anne such a connection to Avonlea, Montgomery reveals the way place can fire the imagination, and imagination, in turn, is what enables a skinny red-haired girl not only to survive but to thrive. It's no wonder that so many people associate the landscape of Prince Edward Island with transformative, nurturing power.

I put my arm around a lichened old spruce and laid my cheek against its rough side—it seemed like an old friend.

—*THE SELECTED JOURNALS OF L. M. MONTGOMERY,* VOL. 1

In the journals she kept throughout her life, Maud Montgomery reveals so many similar experiences to those of Anne Shirley that much of the novel appears to be autobiographical. Even so, she insists that Anne was not based on anyone she knew. "I have *never* drawn any of the characters in my books 'from life,'" she writes, "although I may have taken a quality here and an incident there. I have used real places and speeches freely but I have never put any person I knew into my books." Yet her journals suggest that she is overlooking the most significant influence, for it's clear that the life that most shaped the beloved Anne is the author's own; she herself was the inspiration for the spirited girl whom readers came to love.

Montgomery may have believed that Anne's characteristics were different enough from her own to deflect a sense of personal story—Anne's particularly awful childhood (the author was never in an orphanage), the curse of red hair (the author's was brown), kindly elders to raise her (the author's were not), and the letter "e" as part of her name ("I never liked Lucy as a name,"

Montgomery writes in her journal. "I always liked Maud—spelled not 'with an e' if you please."). And she may have believed that other, obvious similarities lacked significance—both had potted geraniums named "Bonny"; both had the same names for their favorite haunts (the Lake of Shining Waters, Lover's Lane, the Haunted Wood, the Birch Path); both had the same imaginary friends reflected in clear glass—Katie Maurice, Violetta; and both lived with women who were known for their red currant wine.

Or perhaps Montgomery *did* see the common themes of their lives but chose never to admit that to anyone, including herself.

 When I am asked if Anne herself is a "real person" I always answer "no" with an odd reluctance and an uncomfortable feeling of not telling the truth. For she is and always has been, from the moment I first thought of her, so real to me that I feel I am doing violence to something when I deny her an existence anywhere save in Dreamland . . . She *is* so real that, although I've never met her, I feel quite sure I shall do so some day—perhaps in a stroll through Lover's Lane in the twilight—or in the moonlit Birch Path—I shall lift my eyes and find her, child or maiden, by my side. And I shall not be in the least surprised because I have always known she was *somewhere*.

In ways that matter most to readers of the novel, that "*somewhere*" resides solidly within the author's very being. Like Anne Shirley, Maud Montgomery valued the imagination almost as much as life itself. Like Anne, she deliberately chose to emphasize beauty—desiring, always, both to see it and to make it. And perhaps most important, like Anne, she found solace and sustenance in the natural world. The love they express for Prince Edward Island—its farms and forests, its flowers and fields, its past and its people—has imprinted the region on the novel's readers, allowing

29

Late summer goldenrod
(*Solidago* species)

us to believe that, in a place of extraordinary beauty, we, too, can learn to access the best parts of ourselves.

MAUD MONTGOMERY WAS BORN in the town of Clifton (now New London), Prince Edward Island, in November 1874; twenty-one months later, she lost her mother, Clara Woolner Macneill Montgomery, to tuberculosis. Shortly afterward, her father, Hugh John Montgomery, joined the migration of families from Prince Edward Island to western Canada (a journey also taken by

30

Hay bales in a field near Green Gables.

Gilbert Blythe's father), leaving two-year-old Maud in Cavendish with his wife's parents, Alexander and Lucy Macneill. Though she and her father corresponded, Maud would not see him again until she was nine, when he returned to Prince Edward Island for several months. At age twelve, when she learned that he was to be married, she was thrilled—"a real mother to love and be loved by!" She wrote her stepmother, Mary Ann McRae, adoring letters, enclosing pressed flowers gathered from her favorite places. "It gave me exquisite joy," she wrote in her journal years later, "to search the

31

A rear view of the house that Maud Montgomery immortalized as Green Gables, home of her Macneill cousins, siblings David and Margaret, and later of Ernest Webb and his family; now the historic site visited annually by tourists.

woodlands until I found something I deemed perfect enough to offer her." But her hopes were crushed when the two met. Her father's new wife proved to be shallow, mean-spirited, and jealous of the young Maud's hold on her husband's affections, which left Maud as motherless as Anne, soon to return to Prince Edward Island to be raised by grandparents who shared none of her spirit or fire.

But unlike Anne Shirley, Maud Montgomery had a large extended family on the island and her grandparents frequently housed boarders—relatives, summer visitors, teachers from the

Maud Montgomery's father, Hugh John Montgomery.

Maud Montgomery's mother, Clara Macneill Montgomery.

The house where Maud Montgomery was born in Clifton (now New London), Prince Edward Island.

Wedding of Maud
Montgomery's father,
Hugh John Montgomery,
and stepmother, Mary
Ann McRae Montgomery,
1887.

nearby school, the captain of the shipwrecked *Marco Polo*—with most guests adding a welcome vitality to the household. Yet some of her relatives seemed so critical of her that she couldn't seem to do anything to please them. ("My childish faults and short comings—of which I had plenty—were all detailed to the Macneill uncles and aunts whenever they came to the house," she writes, and "I resented this more bitterly than anything else.") Maud's grandfather, in particular, though she described him as a "lover of nature" and possessing "a rich, poetic mind [and] a keen intelligence," was also "a stern, domineering, irritable man," and Maud claimed she always feared him. Throughout her early life, "He bruised my childish feelings in every possible way and inflicted on my girlish pride humiliations whose scars are branded into my very soul." That Matthew Cuthbert emerges as the polar opposite—in his advocacy (puffed sleeves!), his indulgences (the new dress!), and overt fondness ("It's terrible lonesome downstairs without you")—comes as little surprise. In giving Anne this tender "kindred spirit," as she describes him, to help champion her whims and opinions, Montgomery helps reveal another side of the impetuous girl who often proved so puzzling to Marilla.

Montgomery's grandmother was just as different from Marilla as her grandfather was from Matthew. While Marilla is able to adapt to change and apologize when she errs, Maud's

35

Maud Montgomery, her grandparents Lucy and Alexander Macneill, and her Uncle Leander, at their home in Cavendish, Prince Edward Island, 1895.

grandmother was intolerant and set in her ways (at least in the young Maud's eyes) and seemed incapable of showing any affection for the impulsive, sensitive child. Though she was, Montgomery admits, "kind . . . in a material way," in that her granddaughter was "well-cared-for, well-fed, and well-dressed," the two were often at loggerheads, "dissimilar in every respect essential to mutual comfort." In addition to seeming cold and reserved, Maud's grandmother insisted on a way of doing things that Maud described as torture. "I was constantly reproached with ingratitude and wickedness because in childhood, before I had learned any self-control or understanding of my position, I sometimes rebelled against 'her' ways." Of her grandparents, she writes, "Emotionally they grew old before their time, getting into a rut of feeling and living which suited them but was utterly unfitted to

Maud's grandparents' Cavendish home served as the local post office; here, the mailman—pictured in front of the barn—is delivering mail, c. 1890s.

I was impulsive, warm-hearted, emotional; grandmother was cold and reserved, narrow in her affections and sensibilities.

—*THE SELECTED JOURNALS OF L. M. MONTGOMERY, VOL. 1*

RIGHT A line of wind- and salt-battered trees next to a mown field reveals some of the challenges for farmers of the island.

BELOW Schoolchildren outside the Cavendish school, c. 1890s.

anyone who was yet growing in soul or body. It is a great misfortune for a child to be brought up by old people."

In giving the Cuthberts their mix of traits—the silent, adoring Matthew and the pragmatic yet understanding Marilla—Montgomery provides Anne a path for taking on much of her own self-improvement in positive, endearing ways. The siblings help guide her through a series of humorous situations that readers know well (letting her best friend get drunk on red currant wine; dying her red hair green; breaking her ankle while walking the roof beam over the Barrys' kitchen), with Anne determining after each mishap to be brave and try to act differently. Marilla had only

38

to be fair, and Matthew steady and kind, for the emotional girl to learn to rein in some of her wilder impulses.

IN THE SUMMER OF 1890, when Maud was fifteen, she took the train with her grandfather Montgomery to Prince Albert, in Saskatchewan, for an extended stay with her father. Maud's hopes for a glorious reunion with her father were quickly dashed as he could show little overt affection for her, given the jealousies of his new wife. (In a sign of the distance between them, Maud called her "Mrs. Montgomery"—"I *cannot* call her anything except before others for father's sake"; she also wrote in her journal that children avoided

39

A typical Prince Edward Island red road under a canopy of trees.

the house because her stepmother "is so cross," though she risked having the words seen because Mrs. Montgomery "reads all my letters and everything else she can find in my room when I am out.") Maud attended the local school for part of the year but in March was pulled out so she could help her stepmother with housework and the care of the new baby. The experience was painful and gave the young Maud ample material for the stories she would later provide of Anne's years spent working in families with small children before being sent to the orphanage in Nova Scotia.

"The truth of the matter," Maud wrote after a miserable illness, "is I've been working like a slave for the past eight months and I've just gone beyond my strength. I've had to do all the work of this house, except the washing, and help tend the baby, besides, while Mrs. Montgomery walks the streets or visits with relatives." She tried not to complain overtly though, as her father had admitted "that he finds it hard to get along with his wife and asked me to put up with some things for his sake."

"Father is a poor man today," the young Maud wrote about his financial circumstances. "Yet he is one of those men who are loved by everyone. And I—I love him with all my heart—better than anyone else in the whole world—dear, darling father!" With her love for him as a guiding force, Maud endured the chores and her stepmother's relentless criticisms and managed to form strong friendships with several classmates that lasted years after she withdrew from the school, suggesting she possessed the

41

same kind of charisma that made Anne Shirley so popular with her peers.

During these difficult months, and whenever homesickness sets in, memories of Prince Edward Island helped buoy Maud's spirits, transporting her to the landscape that restored her. Less than a week after her arrival, she admitted to her journal, "I have fought it off as long as I could but to-day I succumbed and had a fierce cry all to myself. I'd give anything to see dear old Cavendish for half an hour. Oh, for a glimpse of the old hills and woods and shore!"

Four months later, in December, the feelings surface again, made more acute by the unwanted attentions of the schoolmaster, Mr. Mustard. "Oh, for one glimpse of Cavendish!," she wrote.

 Of course I know it is winter down there now, just as here, but in thinking of it I always remember it just as I left it in the prime of summer with buttercups and asters blooming by the brooks, ferns blowing spicily in the woods, lazy sunshine sleeping on the hills, with the beautiful sea beyond blue and bright and far-reaching. There is no spot on earth more lovely.

In addition to their shared orphan status, Maud Montgomery recorded many additional elements in her journals, both before and after her return to Prince Edward Island, that she would later weave into Anne Shirley's life. Both loved learning and attended similarly described schools; both adored books and memorized favorite passages and long poems; both attended "concerts"—public recitations and performances—whenever possible, and both mesmerized audiences when it came their time to contribute to the evening's entertainment. In addition, both were ambitious and competitive in proving mastery of their lessons, and both ranked far above their peers in the entrance exams for the college in Charlottetown (while Montgomery ranked fifth

42

"THEY LOOKED AT HER AND WHISPERED TO EACH OTHER."

The girls in church, their hats adorned with ribbons and artificial flowers, laughed as the new girl, Anne, appeared wearing one she had decorated with "wind-stirred buttercups and a glory of wild roses." Illustration by M. A. and W. A. J. Claus, from the 1908 edition.

in the province, she added tension to the novel's plot by having Anne and Gilbert tie for first).

But the most important similarities between Maud of the journals and Anne of Green Gables are those that evoke both passion and solace—an infectious delight in the natural world, a friendship with wild things, a sense of comfort and spiritual renewal in life outdoors, and a belief in the transformative power of the landscape's splendor.

NUMEROUS PASSAGES IN *Anne of Green Gables* and in the additional *Anne* novels appeared first as entries in Maud Montgomery's journals. She took pains in crafting scenes, whether transcribing conversations or waxing "poetical" about her surroundings, and she vented such raw feelings—joy and rage, indignation and awe—that when Anne was in the throes of a similar emotion, the material was already there on the page to give to the garrulous girl. One such example is the mayflower picnic beloved by both Maud and Anne, when the students would head out from school on a clear day in May and gather armfuls of the fragrant blossoms—"pink and white stars of sweetness under their brown leaves"—to wreath around their hats and carry in bouquets as they sang their way back home.

"I long for the sight of them," Montgomery wrote in her journal, "little pale pilgrims from summerland . . . when we went rambling through 'the barrens' . . . coming upon plots of them, sweet and fragrant and shy, hidden away in the spruce nooks and hollows." Anne described them to Marilla in equally

Anne felt passionately about mayflowers (*Epigaea repens*). "I think it would be *tragic*," she tells Marilla in *Anne of Green Gables*, "not to know what Mayflowers are like."

Horse and buggy traverse a Prince Edward Island road.

glowing terms, claiming that mayflowers "must be the souls of the flowers that died last summer and this is their heaven."

From the very first sentence of *Anne of Green Gables*, readers are introduced to the idea that natural things—brooks, flowers, trees—are, to both Maud Montgomery and Anne Shirley, animate. The brook that runs past Rachel Lynde's house flows from its source with a headlong rush, though it knows to slow down and be "a quiet, well-conducted little stream" when passing Mrs. Lynde's, as though it were conscious of the older woman's penchant for ferreting out mischief-makers.

45

Queen Anne's lace (*Daucus carota*) in front of the pond in Park Corner, Prince Edward Island, the inspiration for Montgomery's Lake of Shining Waters.

A few pages later, when Anne is finally in the buggy with Matthew, en route at last to Green Gables, she lavishes attention on things she sees as having spirits of their own; she bids good-night to the newly named Lake of Shining Waters ("I always say good night to the things I love, just as I would to people. I think they like it"); and, just before arriving at Green Gables, she hears the voices of the trees "talking in their sleep" and imagines the "dreams they must have!"

Within a day of her arrival, she gives names to Marilla's geranium (Bonny) and to the flowering cherry tree outside her window (Snow Queen). Within a few more days, she has come to know all the shrubs and trees around the house and "made friends with the spring down in the hollow." And upon returning from her first church service in Avonlea, she waves in greeting to Bonny and to a nearby fuchsia, knowing they might have "been lonesome" when she was gone.

Here, too, Montgomery was drawing on her own experience. "I just love the woods," she wrote in her journal at age fourteen. Seventeen years later, she elaborated a bit more: "In the woods I like to be alone for every tree is a true old friend and every tiptoeing wind a merry comrade. If I believed seriously in the doctrine of transmigration I should think I had been a *tree* in some previous stage of existence."

"Anne's habit of naming things," wrote Montgomery, "was an old one of my own giving romantic names to cherished

47

Lover's Lane, c. 1895, colorized by Maud Montgomery in the 1920s.

A view down Lover's Lane today.

places." The names that Anne and Montgomery used for many of these places are identical, making it easy for readers to move from the world of fiction to the actual, physical world of Prince Edward Island. Anne's Lover's Lane, she wrote, "was of course *my* Lover's Lane," while the Lake of Shining Waters was based on the pond near her relatives' home at Park Corner (though in "the effects of light and shadow," she admitted, the nearby Cavendish Pond probably influenced her as well). The idea for the Birch Path came from a photograph that had appeared in *Outing* magazine,

50

The Lake of Shining Waters with its wood-plank bridge, Park Corner, c. 1895; colorized by Maud Montgomery in the 1920s.

though she had ample groves of birches to draw on for their comforting shape and pale aspect. Other names—Willowmere, Violet Vale, the Dryad's Bubble—were invented for the novel, but the Haunted Wood was a place she knew well, along with "the old log bridge" near Green Gables, which she crossed often.

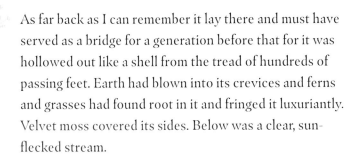

As far back as I can remember it lay there and must have served as a bridge for a generation before that for it was hollowed out like a shell from the tread of hundreds of passing feet. Earth had blown into its crevices and ferns and grasses had found root in it and fringed it luxuriantly. Velvet moss covered its sides. Below was a clear, sunflecked stream.

51

In addition to being a source of beauty and wonder, the natural world also provides Maud and Anne a spiritual home. "If I really wanted to pray," Anne tells Marilla, "I'd go out into a great big field all alone or into the deep, deep woods, and I'd look up into the sky—up—up—up—into that lovely blue sky that looks as if there was no end to its blueness. And then I'd just *feel* a prayer." Montgomery echoed this sentiment in her journal (a scene that she develops further when imagining the perfect place for a wedding—the kind that Anne and Gilbert will ultimately have in *Anne's House of Dreams*):

 I have an ideal Sunday in my mind. Only, I am such a coward that I cannot translate it into the real but must drift on with the current of conventionality . . . But I would like to go away on Sunday morning to the heart of some great solemn wood and sit down among the ferns with only the companionship of the trees and the wood-winds echoing through the dim, moss-hung aisles like the strains of some vast cathedral anthem. And I would stay there for hours alone with nature and my own soul.

It's to the natural world, then, that each girl turns when her soul is beginning to despair. The inspiration found there not only shifts her mood, it changes the very caliber of the writing, the sentences seemingly possessed of a new vitality, bringing readers

Ferns by a stream on a trail near Lover's Lane.

into a brighter, better place. An early example from Montgomery's journal, written during the drudgery of the annual potato harvest, has young Maud and her friend ending the day in "tattered, beclayed old dresses," their "faces plastered with dirt and mud." But rather than dwell in her writing on the grime or physical weariness, she turns instead to the stunning view just beyond.

> We were picking potatoes all day up in our hill field ... I hate it! But since pick I had to I was glad it was up in the hill field because I love that field. There is such a glorious view from it—the deep blue sea, the pond as blue as a sapphire, the groves of maple and birch just turning to scarlet and gold, the yellow stubble-lands and the sere pastures.

Later, in an angry entry written while in Saskatchewan, she vented about the rough way her stepmother had treated and dismissed a hired girl named Edie. "It has been a dismal day," Maud wrote. "I feel so lonely." She recounted her stepmother's "vile temper," her jealousy of Edie and Maud's friendship, and the awkward position Mrs. Montgomery put Edie in. "It has made me feel absolute contempt for her," Maud wrote. But then, rather than elaborate on her fractious relationship with Mrs. Montgomery, she shifted instead to a subject that soothed her—a letter she had received from home containing dried poppies and pansies. "It just seemed as if they spoke to me and whispered a loving message of

55

A field in Cavendish, c. 1890.

Hollyhocks (*Alcea rosea*) in bloom near Green Gables.

a far-off land where blue skies are bending over maple-crimsoned hills and spruce glens are still green and dim in their balsamic recesses." Both the memory of Cavendish and the language she used to honor it exerted a calming effect, and the anger at Mrs. Montgomery slowly abated.

In the early days of Anne's time at Green Gables, a similar transformation can be seen taking hold of Anne—much to Marilla's surprise. After being told to hold her tongue, as she talked "entirely too much for a little girl," Anne settles into

57

silence, becoming "more and more abstracted, eating mechanically, with her big eyes fixed . . . on the sky outside the window." Marilla hardly knows what to make of the change, for "while this odd child's body might be there at the table her spirit was far away in some remote airy cloudland, borne aloft on the wings of imagination."

It's an exquisite moment for all that it reveals about the power of an active inner life to lift an individual out of her immediate circumstances. Throughout the novel, Anne's imagination flourishes in the beauty of the natural world in a way that invites us all to pay it closer attention, and to take advantage, whenever possible, of its potential to help us transform the moments that regularly challenge our own lives.

The "White Lady," a favorite tree of Maud Montgomery,
c. 1890; colorized by Montgomery in the 1920s.

For lands have personalities just as well as human beings; and to know that personality you must live in the land and companion it, and draw sustenance of body and spirit from it; so only can you really know a land and be known of it.

—THE ALPINE PATH

THE LOVELIEST SPOT ON EARTH

PRINCE EDWARD ISLAND
THEN AND NOW

Travelers heading to Prince Edward Island to experience the transformative power of Anne's and Maud's landscapes will find, at first glance, a very different world from the one that they inhabited. A bridge and airport now make travel on and off island easy; cars cruise the roads at 60 miles per hour; and the commercial stretches, especially on the approach to Cavendish, can make Anne's dreamy rural world seem lost in the distant past. Yet despite the obvious changes—large mechanized farm equipment instead of horse-drawn plows and wagons; brightly colored theme parks where crops once grew; paved roads in place of red-dirt lanes—the essential character of Prince Edward Island remains the same. The wave-etched cliffs along Cavendish Beach, the woods of fern-lined brooks and mossy stretches, the gently sloping fields with a sea of infinite blue just beyond greet the visitor as they did Anne Shirley, when arriving full of hope that here she would find the home where she might be wanted at last.

Hay bales near the home where Montgomery lived with her grandparents.

That Anne's land is an island is a big reason for its enduring nature. About 140 miles long and 40 miles across at its widest, Prince Edward Island is defined as much by the sea as by its quiet inland beauty. Even when the ocean can't be seen, its presence can be felt, providing a sense of both containment and separation for island residents. Dip down into a valley where the waters are invisible and the air is moist, the temperatures moderated, the breezes carrying hints of the sea's smells and sounds. Wander to a hilltop or venture close to the shore and the cry of gulls, the lap of waves, and the creak of moored boats are as present as they were in Anne's day. Or head to the shore where the Gulf Stream flows so near the coast that the summer waters are warm enough for swimming, the beaches inviting and long, and the slope of white and red sand dunes gentle enough to create a sense of an idyllic, unlikely northern island.

Before the bridge to the mainland was completed in 1997 (the longest in the world over water that freezes), travel on and off the island was by boat, though even the ice-breaking ferries couldn't guarantee passage in the winter. This left the island, already at a considerable distance from major airports and commercial hubs, dependent on the natural resilience of its inhabitants. Farming and fishing persist as the economic mainstays (with Prince Edward Island oysters and potatoes enjoying far-flung reputations), while the beaches, golf courses, and popularity of Montgomery's novels keep tourism an important, albeit seasonal, source of income.

65

On the surface, change on the island seems to have moved at the pace of Matthew's buggy after collecting Anne at the train station for her first night at Green Gables. Electricity, indoor plumbing, and telephones in private homes arrived later than on the mainland, while one-room schoolhouses for first through eighth grade continued into the 1970s.

The long rectangles of farmed land, outlined by tall dark spruces or pines, suggest a design that hasn't changed since the original sixty-seven plots were drawn by Britain, after expelling the French Acadians in the late eighteenth century. Unfortunately, the lottery system they used to entice would-be settlers to the island drew speculators instead, beginning a long history of absentee owners. The resulting lack of local engagement caused considerable unrest, but it also meant little deviation from the original grids. It wasn't until the Compulsory Land Purchase Act in 1873 that the distant landowners were forced to sell, a resolution that allowed Prince Edward Island to host—and then join—the Canadian Confederation of provinces. The historic conference, held in Charlottetown in 1864, gave rise to two of Prince Edward Island's nicknames—"Birthplace of Confederation" and "Cradle of Confederation"—and to the names of significant local places, including the eight-mile-long Confederation Bridge; the 290-mile-long Confederation Trail, a bike path that runs the length of the island along the old railway lines; and the stunning Confederation Centre of the Arts in downtown Charlottetown.

Other changes to the island came more quickly. The precariousness of livelihoods, where winters are long, hard freezes and droughts can wipe out crops, and fishing open waters comes with all kinds of risks, prompted many islanders to head west in search of easier work and higher returns. The number of family-owned farms fell from roughly 10,000 at mid-century to closer to 1600 today, most of them consolidated into the large agribusinesses. At the same time, a big drop in traditional fish stocks (and the moratorium on cod that began in 1992) forced many families to give up

66

THE LOVELIEST SPOT ON EARTH

A postcard from the PEI Museum and Heritage
Foundation shows haying in Montgomery's time.

Protected dunes, Cavendish Beach, Prince Edward Island National Park.

The timeless look of Prince Edward Island fields.

their boats and find other work. At the beginning of the twentieth century, when Maud Montgomery was writing her first novel, the population stood at about 100,000; during the Depression years, it dropped to a low of about 86,000 but has since risen to roughly 140,000 today.

Accompanying these changes are those that reveal the adaptability of the islanders. Many areas were converted to blueberries, a popular cash crop, while the sheltered bays began to fill with new forms of aquaculture, primarily oyster and mussel farms, which are visible as lines of black buoys that float atop long mesh tubes, each filled with hundreds of the tiny young bivalves.

The Literary and Village Improvement Societies of Anne's day, along with the concerts and church socials, have given way to music festivals, summer theater, and the popular ceilidhs (pronounced *kay*-lees) or "kitchen parties" of Celtic music and dance. Craftspeople continue to find new niches for their work, and farmer's markets bring together growers and consumers interested in the value-added products that allow the smaller farms to survive.

Similar changes have taken place on the land itself, where abandoned farms gave way to weeds; shrubs and orchards disappeared into the scrub; and trees grow old and die or are harvested for timber, as happened to the original Haunted Wood and to Idlewild, site of Anne and Diana Barry's playhouse ("Mr. Bell having ruthlessly cut down the little circle of trees in his back pasture in the spring"). Lupine, a tall multi-hued roadside flower,

70

arrived after Montgomery's first novel was published; its spires of blossoms now provide an array of summer color, while its presence has become ubiquitous on Prince Edward Island photos and postcards.

By 1900, most of the original forests were gone, along with many of the large mammals that once inhabited them, including black bear, caribou, and moose. (Deer never established themselves on the island, though coyotes have recently arrived, presumably crossing over from the mainland when the straits were covered in ice.) In a reversal of the earlier land-clearing trend, about half of the island is forested today, much of it in trees that are often young and evenly aged. On a walk through the woods, it's not unusual to find daylilies and lilacs that mark an abandoned homestead, and apple trees that bear fruit in the middle of a new pine forest.

71

An early apple in the orchard at Silver Bush, the Park Corner home of Montgomery's Campbell relatives.

Given these cyclical, inevitable changes, it's even more remarkable that the sites devoted to keeping Anne Shirley's story alive—the house and grounds of Green Gables; the adjoining homesite, where Montgomery grew up; and Silver Bush in Park Corner, where her dear Campbell relatives lived and where the Anne of Green Gables Museum now stands—can maintain their timeless feel. The custodians of these places—the National Park Service and the descendants of the Macneill and Campbell

Green Gables today.

families—have worked wonders in preserving these windows into the lives and the land of Anne's Avonlea.

Theirs is not an easy task. Not only do they have to maintain a sense of late-nineteenth-century life in a twenty-first-century world, they also have to walk a very thin line between the real world of Maud Montgomery and the fictional world so vividly inhabited by Anne and Diana and Gilbert, and by Marilla and Matthew and Rachel Lynde. Such finessing is most visible at

73

One of the two pantries at Green Gables.

Dinnerware in a pantry off the kitchen at Green Gables.

the beautifully maintained house, Green Gables, and on the surrounding acres. It can be tough to remember that the Haunted Wood seen today is not the same woods of Maud's and Anne's time, nor is Lover's Lane the same lane, nor the orchards the ones that framed Anne's view out her upstairs window. Even the house has evolved over the years—the original shingles replaced by clapboards, the second story extended over the kitchen, and electricity brought in, relegating candles and lamps to sideboards or closets.

And yet the rooms appear furnished exactly as Anne Shirley knew them—the bedrooms look as though their occupants just left for the day; the utensils in the kitchen appear ready for the next meal; and the stairs Anne and the Cuthberts went up and down still resonate with the sound of those earlier feet. From

Anne's room at Green Gables.

Woman in period costume at Green Gables.

TOP Marilla's room at Green Gables.

LEFT Matthew's room at Green Gables.

the vintage clothing and furniture to the geraniums in the windows, the house seems to embody the years when Anne's essence completely filled it.

For visitors keen to see how the land influenced Maud Montgomery, and how she, in turn, celebrated its significance in her work, a good introduction to the area is to save Green Gables for later in the tour and head first to the site of the home that Maud

77

The back orchard of Maud Montgomery's grandparents'
house, c. 1890s. Photograph by L. M. Montgomery.

Dry-stacked stone foundation on the site of the former Macneill house, where Maud Montgomery lived with her grandparents.

Montgomery shared with her grandparents. Today, only the foundation remains of the house where she lived for over half her life, a further reminder of the years that have passed since she stared out the windows, outlined Anne's adventures, and kept her manuscript well hidden from visitors, many of whom were arriving for their mail, as the house also served as the local post office. Standing near the old cellar hole, it's easy to imagine the smells of the orchard in bloom, the sight of cows seeking shade, or the sounds of the trees, "always rustling and whispering to you."

Roses near the old Macneill homestead.

The trail leading from the old homestead to the Haunted Wood and Green Gables.

Jewelweed—what Anne called ladies' eardrops—alongside the Haunted Wood trail.

OPPOSITE A geranium in the window at Green Gables; Anne gave the name "Bonny" to Marilla's apple-scented geranium.

A tree-lined trail, suggesting one that Anne and Diana might have used, heads away from the old foundation, crosses the main road, and enters the well-marked Haunted Wood. From here to Green Gables, signs inscribed with lines from Montgomery's writings evoke the intimate relationship both she and Anne felt with the land. ("I consider it a misfortune to love any place as I love this old homestead . . . the agony of parting from it is intolerable"; "I love this old home deeply . . . and I love Cavendish.") Depending on the day and the traffic, or the decision to wander slowly or hurry on to the bigger attraction, the trail can provide the same smells of earth and pine, the same play of light and shadow, the same moist air above the stream that both knew and loved.

Entering Green Gables from this direction offers a clearer threshold between the real world of Maud Montgomery and the fictional world of Anne Shirley. Once inside Anne's home, it's easy to see a geranium as an old friend ("Bonny!"), or sense the young orphan's fear when she wasn't sure if she'd be allowed to stay, or witness her fury at Rachel Lynde for noting how skinny she was and homely and so very red-haired.

"'I HATE YOU,' SHE CRIED IN A CHOKED VOICE, STAMPING
HER FOOT ON THE FLOOR."

Anne's fury at Rachel Lynde; "'I hate you,' she cried in a choked
voice, stamping her foot on the floor." Illustration by M. A. and
W. A. J. Claus, from the 1908 edition.

Outside the house, another well-marked trail takes visitors down Lover's Lane, past sun-warmed roses, and alongside a tall stand of birches. To many readers, this stretch of the island will feel like hallowed ground, as Montgomery loved Lover's Lane "idolatrously" and felt "happier there than anywhere else." She celebrated its beauty in all seasons and knew to seek it out as a cure for her sorrows. "It is the dearest spot in the world to me," she wrote in an 1899 journal entry, "and has the greatest influence for good over me. No matter how dark my mood is, no matter how heavy my heart . . . an hour in that beautiful solitude will put me right with myself and the world."

The Balsam Hollow Trail, a spur off Lover's Lane, winds through spruce and fir trees, a remnant of the earlier Acadian forest. A quiet stream runs through it, evoking images of the hours the children of Avonlea spent trouting or plucking spruce gum from tree trunks (when still pliable, the bits of golden resin can be chewed like gum) or dipping twigs in balsam pitch for the rainbows they made on still water.

In spring, woodland flowers carpet the ground. In late summer and fall, Canada dogwood's orange-red berries—what Anne calls pigeon berries—stand out against the dark greens of the conifers around them. Also known as bunchberry, Canada dogwood often grows in these Acadian forests alongside starflower, twinflower (June bells in the novels), Canada mayflower or wild lily of the valley (Anne calls them rice lilies), and yellow

Balsam pitch on the end of a twig creates a rainbow effect when in water.

bluebead-lily or clintonia. In any season, if the day is clear or the clouds open, the light that comes through the boughs overhead sifts "through so many emerald screens that it [is] as flawless as the heart of a diamond."

After leaving Green Gables, another interesting site can be found a short drive to the west on Route 6. Avonlea Village, designed to provide visitors a sense of Anne Shirley's community, reveals many of the architectural features of buildings from her era. While most are replicas, two notable original buildings were moved to the site: the schoolhouse where Maud Montgomery taught in Belmont from 1896 to 1897, and the Presbyterian church from Long River, which she attended when visiting relatives at Park Corner (the building had to be cut into four pieces

Maud Montgomery's photograph captures a grove of
birch trees near the trouting pond, c. 1890s.

Ferns alongside a stream on the Balsam Hollow Trail.

Several of the buildings in Avonlea Village were moved to the site; others were designed to replicate period houses.

to be moved). For years, craftspeople in period costume engaged in activities of Anne's time; the site now functions as a place of shops and restaurants.

For an ideal ending to such a day, it's worth a drive down the road to the National Park's Cavendish Beach, perhaps holding in mind the way it looked to Anne when she first saw the view—red cliffs and white sand with the sea straight ahead, "shimmering and blue, and over it soared the gulls, their pinions flashing silvery in the sunlight." Boardwalks cross the dunes at regular intervals, providing access to the miles-long beach and the wind- and sea-carved cliffs.

89

Red cliffs of Cavendish Beach.

Members of the Campbell family along the north shore of Prince Edward Island, c. 1890s. Photograph by L. M. Montgomery.

After strolling the beach or climbing the sandstone formations, visitors can have a quieter, more shaded walk on the trail behind the dunes, along the adjacent wetlands and cattail-lined marshes. The trail eventually reaches the large Macneill Pond (also known as Cavendish Pond)—the other body of water that Montgomery had in mind when envisioning the Lake of Shining Waters (the main influence was the Campbells' pond at Park Corner).

For a fuller immersion into Anne's and Maud's worlds, it's worth devoting a second day to a tour of Montgomery's birthplace in New London (called Clifton at the time of her birth) and Silver Bush, in the town of Park Corner, where her cousins and dear Uncle John and Aunt Annie Campbell lived, and where their

91

The trail behind the dunes, Cavendish Beach.

descendants continue to maintain the Anne of Green Gables Museum. The first of these, looking as it might have during the first two years of the author's life, displays such artifacts as the dress Montgomery was married in and the shoes she wore for the ceremony, along with several of her early scrapbooks. The labels and careful arrangements (all in Montgomery's hand) reflect her awareness of the growing interest in everything about her, and her desire to shape the way that information was presented.

Maud Montgomery's bedroom for the first two years of her life, before her mother's death.

TOP The house in New London (formerly called Clifton), where Maud Montgomery was born on November 30, 1874.

On the northwestern side of New London Bay is Silver Bush, where Maud Montgomery spent some of her happiest years—the house, the barn, the orchard, and the Lake of Shining Waters. Visitors to the house can find rooms full of photographs, handwritten letters framed and on the walls, and a breakfront with the reminder that it was in just such a reflection that Anne (and Maud) conversed with their imagined companions. Here, too, one can ride a horse-pulled wagon driven by a Matthew Cuthbert

93

A look across the Campbells' pond, which Montgomery named the Lake of Shining Waters.

look-alike and walk by the lake in its various moods and meditative moments.

While the landscapes of Cavendish and Park Corner provide the setting for *Anne of Green Gables* (and the later novels *Pat of Silver Bush* and *Mistress Pat*), for more insight into Maud Montgomery's life, a journey west to Prince County then down to Lower Bedeque is well worth the drive to see the areas where

Carriage rides with a Matthew look-alike are offered around the grounds and the pond.

Montgomery taught school, where she became engaged to Edwin Simpson, where she struggled with terrible loneliness, and where she fell in love with another man, eventually breaking off her first engagement.

At the first of her teaching appointments, in Bideford, on the far west end of Malpeque Bay, she boarded with the Esteys in a Victorian home that's open to visitors today. In some ways, the

A plaque outside Silver Bush, home of Montgomery's Campbell relatives, identifies the importance of the place to her. "I love this old spot," she wrote in a letter to her cousin Donald Campbell, "better than any place on earth."

year was a surprising success for her—"the last happy year of my life," she wrote in 1910, after spending a day thinking about her "whole past life." Further evidence of her emotional state is suggested by what is *not* in her journals, as this was a period of time when she wasn't crafting lengthy, lyrical descriptions of the land to buoy her spirits; in Bideford, teaching took her full attention and the social whirl delighted her.

During her time in Bideford, she saved enough money from her salary (with additional support from her grandmother)

The Campbell home in Park Corner, c. 1890s.
Photograph by L. M. Montgomery.

A low-lying shore typical of much of Prince Edward Island.

The schoolhouse at Lower Bedeque.

to spend the subsequent year at the Halifax Ladies College (now Dalhousie University) in Halifax, Nova Scotia. There, she took as many courses as she could to help advance her desire of becoming a better writer. Her funds only covered the single year, however, at which point she had to resort to another year of teaching, this time in Belmont, on the southern shore of Malpeque Bay. (The old one-room schoolhouse has since been moved to Avonlea Village in Cavendish.) Student needs, lonely hours, the constant cold in the room where she boarded (she writes of waking to snow on her pillow) marked the year as "the hardest I ever lived . . . in almost every way a year could be hard."

A drive through the region reveals a scrubbier land than the lush hills of Cavendish, the soil poorer, the exposure more harsh—as Montgomery notes in her journal, when aching for a place to walk, "no leafy lanes, no secluded fields . . . The only place is the bay shore and that is rather damp and boggy just now." She seemed to shiver day and night; she struggled with her teaching load and the pinched social setting; and, lonely and facing an uncertain future, she finally relented to Edwin Simpson's entreaties and became engaged to him.

100

Her final year as a teacher was spent in Lower Bedeque, in the southwestern corner of Prince County near where the Dunk River flows into Bedeque Bay, and Prince Edward Island is narrowest. Here, everything seems more fertile, the prevailing winds gentler, the community more welcoming. A historical site commemorates this period of her life—which was also marked by a love affair with Herman Leard and personal torment about misleading Ed Simpson—with a restored one-room schoolhouse, complete with original outhouse, hand pump, and line-up of tin cups. Of this time she simply writes, "A year of mad passion!"

It would take her months, though she might have said years, to recover from the affair and the dissolution of the engagement,

Inside the schoolhouse, restored in 1989 and now a museum.

Sunset at Cavendish Beach.

though it was the death of her grandfather during that tumultuous time, in March of 1898, that most altered her life. She returned to Cavendish to care for her grandmother, who was then seventy-six, and there she slowly began to recover. A year later, the familiar landscapes had worked their magic.

> It is evening while I am writing. The sun has got down behind the trees and their long, lazy shadows are falling over the lane and fields. Beyond, the brown hills are basking in an amber radiance underneath a pale aerial sky of rose and blue. The firs on the south hill are like burnished bronze and their long shadows are barring the hill meadows. Dear old world, you are very beautiful and I love you well.

Though it would be several more years before she began work on *Anne of Green Gables*, Maud Montgomery's deep love for her dear old Cavendish world had proven restorative, an affection that she would soon channel through a spirited eleven-year-old girl.

103

I had, in my vivid imagination, a passport to the geography of Fairyland. In a twinkling I could—and did—whisk myself into regions of wonderful adventures, unhampered by any restrictions of time or place.

—THE ALPINE PATH

SOMETHING MORE POETICAL

THE SCOPE OF
TWO IMAGINATIONS

For a novel that is as much about a stalwart eleven-year-old as it is about the role of the imagination and the transformative beauty of a particular landscape, it's hard to imagine a more perfect beginning than the circumstances of Anne's arrival. Hailing *from away* (Nova Scotia), Anne Shirley appears as the outsider, ready to be welcomed into a new home, seeing everything with fresh eyes. As she waits at the platform to be picked up by "something or somebody," the first thing we learn about her (other than that she's not a boy) is from the station-master, who tells Matthew that he had encouraged her to sit in the ladies' waiting-room but that "she preferred to stay outside." "There was more scope for imagination," he quotes her as saying. "She's a case, I should say," he adds. In this case: a girl, independent in her actions and placing a greater value on imagination than on comfort or propriety in this place where she doesn't know a soul.

Horses in a field near Park Corner, Prince Edward Island.

OPPOSITE French River, a scenic fishing village on the way to Park Corner, Prince Edward Island.

It's equally hard to imagine a better foil for the work of that imagination than the taciturn Matthew, who, having grown up on the island, never felt a need to question what he sees around him. Anne dazzles him repeatedly—the reader, too—with such observations as her plan to climb a nearby tree and spend the night, had no one come to pick her up—"it would be lovely to sleep in a wild cherry-tree all white with bloom in the moonshine, don't you think?" She continues to startle him on the drive to Green Gables with her almost nonstop, fascinating chatter, punctuated again and again by exclamations on all she sees.

This island is the bloomiest place . . . I always heard that Prince Edward Island was the prettiest place in the world, and I used to imagine I was living here, but I never really expected I would. It's delightful when your imaginations come true, isn't it?

108

Canola, grown for its oil, turns fields yellow when in bloom.

A horse-drawn buggy in front of Green Gables.

She stops only when struck dumb by the view down the Avenue, its canopy of blossoms framing the sunset sky, which "shone like a great rose window at the end of a cathedral aisle." Once recovered from the "queer funny ache" that left her temporarily speechless, she decides to call the stretch of road "the White Way of Delight," and so begins her process of claiming and renaming her new world.

It will be another day before Marilla has a similar glimpse into Anne's imaginative life—when she goes to call her for breakfast the next morning and finds Anne rapturous as she looks out at the blossoming cherry tree and all that lies beyond. "Oh, isn't it wonderful?" Anne asks, which Marilla downplays by emphasizing that the tree produces "small and wormy" fruit.

 Oh, I don't mean just the tree; of course it's lovely—yes, it's *radiantly* lovely—it blooms as if it meant it—but I meant everything, the garden and the orchard and the

110

A red road under a canopy of birch trees.

brook and the woods, the whole big dear world. Don't you feel as if you just loved the world on a morning like this? And I can hear the brook laughing all the way up here. Have you ever noticed what cheerful things brooks are? They're always laughing. Even in winter-time I've heard them under the ice. I'm so glad there's a brook near Green Gables. Perhaps you think it doesn't make any difference to me when you're not going to keep me, but it does. I

111

shall always like to remember that there is a brook at Green Gables even if I never see it again.

The scene sends Anne into an imagined future, where "it was really me you wanted after all and . . . I was to stay here for ever and ever." Marilla, however, torn as she is about what to do with the odd orphan, has little patience for such talk, or for the chatter that Anne launches into over the morning meal. But when she tells Anne to hold her tongue, she's startled by the change that comes over the suddenly silent girl, her spirit so clearly elsewhere that Marilla finds herself doubting that she would want to keep a child with such a fervent imagination in her house.

The moment highlights a characteristic that sets Anne Shirley and Maud Montgomery apart from their peers—the strength, so foreign to Marilla, of the powerful visions that each can willingly summon, and the ongoing dilemma for those who witness the process. But as readers we have already seen the glories that accompany such imaginings and, whether conscious of it or not, we have felt the writing itself change each time the landscape is invoked.

Some of the implements that can be seen at Green Gables—a wooden shovel, a wooden wheelbarrow, and a woven splint basket, used for gathering potatoes during the annual harvest.

Both Maud and Anne are keenly aware of the uniqueness of their imaginations (as when Anne points out, after Diana names the Birch Path, that she "could have found something more poetical"), and both know that having such a power can be a blessing as well as a curse. Much of *Anne of Green Gables* chronicles the scrapes Anne gets into when her imagination takes over, despite her best intentions. When she burns a pie in the oven, she has to explain to Marilla what happened. "I was firmly resolved when you left me in charge this morning, not to imagine anything, but keep my thoughts on facts"; nevertheless, she couldn't resist her imagination's pull into the outside world. "I was trying to think of a name for a new island Diana and I have discovered up the brook. It's the most ravishing spot, Marilla. There are two maple-trees on it and the brook flows right around it."

This intense engagement with the physical landscape, the fantasies it sets in motion, and the way it lifts Anne out of her immediate surroundings, also set the stage for her first confrontation with Gilbert. She is deep in a reverie, as she looks out the schoolroom window at the Lake of Shining Waters, and enters a "gorgeous dreamland, hearing and seeing nothing save her own wonderful visions." Gilbert knows none of this, however; he tugs her braid, calls her "Carrots," and she leaps into action with her slate. He'll pay for his miscalculation for years.

And while it's a dare, not the work of her imagination that has Anne walking the Barrys' roof, it's the latter that saves her after breaking her ankle in the subsequent fall. "Isn't it fortunate I've got such an imagination?" Anne says to Marilla as she begins her recovery. "It will help me through splendidly, I expect. What do people who haven't any imagination do when they break their bones?"

This vivid imagination—and its contagious effect on her friends—plays out again later in the book when she throws herself into the role of Elaine from Tennyson's poem *Idylls of the King*. Anne is so convincing in a black shawl and yellow piano scarf, a blue iris in her folded hands, and so pale and still that it frightens Ruby Gillis. ("Anne," says Jane, "for goodness sake smile a little.") The girls—Ruby, Jane, Diana—then kiss her farewell, push the boat into the water, and rush off to the lower headland, where, as Lancelot, Guinevere, and the King, they will "receive the lily maid." But unbeknownst to them, the boat has almost immediately begun to leak, leaving Anne, without oars, to resort to prayer and a hope that the boat will drift near the bridge. Her plea is answered, she would later tell Mrs. Allan, the minister's wife, and she catches hold of a piling just as the boat sinks, but her

113

"THWACK! ANNE HAD BROUGHT HER SLATE DOWN ON GIL-
BERT'S HEAD."

Anne breaks her slate over Gilbert's head. Illustration by
M. A. and W. A. J. Claus, from the 1908 edition.

"BALANCED HERSELF UPRIGHTLY ON THAT PRECARIOUS
FOOTING."

Anne accepts the dare. Illustration by M. A. and W. A. J.
Claus, from the 1908 edition.

imagination won't let go. "Anne looked at the wicked green depths below her, wavering with long, oily shadows, and shivered . . . [All] manner of gruesome possibilities" suggesting themselves to her. And then—horrors!—the unimaginable happens, and Gilbert Blythe comes to her rescue.

"Will you ever have any sense, Anne?" Marilla asks her later, to which Anne replies that she thinks she will, that she's realized she has to give up being so romantic and living so much in her imagination. (It's Matthew who will help temper her sudden decision. "Don't give up all your romance, Anne," he whispers shyly, "a little of it is a good thing—not too much, of course—but keep a little of it, Anne, keep a little of it.")

The youthful impulse to romanticize—and abruptly swear off it—is another trait that Anne Shirley and Maud Montgomery share, both learning early in their lives that what they saw in their imaginations could easily overshadow actual circumstances. Maud Montgomery recounts several such childhood moments in her journals and in *The Alpine Path*, beginning with an event that happened when she was five, while suffering first from a terribly burnt hand and then from typhoid fever. Her grandmother came to visit when Maud was still delirious, but after leaving the room, her father told the young Maud that her grandmother had gone home. When she returned shortly afterward, Maud refused to believe it, so convinced was she by her father's words and so able to visualize her grandmother elsewhere, that no one could change

116

"HE PULLED CLOSE TO THE PILE AND EXTENDED HIS HAND."

Gilbert's rescue of Anne. Illustration by M. A. and
W. A. J. Claus, from the 1908 edition.

her mind. Her grandmother was there but Maud couldn't see her; it had to be that other woman, Mrs. Murphy, who worked for her grandparents and whom Maud didn't like. Comfort was out of reach; the power of her imagination was too strong. When the truth finally breaks in, "I was so happy," Montgomery writes, that "[I] could not bear to be out of her arms."

In later passages, Montgomery tells about a ghostly presence that terrifies her and her friends but which, they later discover, was simply her grandmother at a distance with a white tablecloth; she also recounts a terror she experiences while alone in the woods, which she uses for Anne's and Diana's subsequent horror about being in the Haunted Wood at night. As Anne tells Marilla of the power their stories have over them:

> Oh, we have imagined the most harrowing things. There's a white lady walks along the brook . . . and wrings her hands and utters wailing cries . . . And the ghost of a little murdered child . . . creeps up behind you and lays its cold fingers on your hand . . . [And] a headless man stalks up and down the path and skeletons glower at you between the boughs.

Marilla has no sympathy for such notions, believing that a walk through the dark wood will cure Anne of such fancies. Though almost paralyzed with terror, Anne does as Marilla bids, and makes it through the woods and back, much of it with her eyes shut, "preferring to take the risk of dashing her brains out among the boughs" than coming face to face with a ghost.

> A white strip of birch bark blowing up from the hollow over the brown floor of the grove made her heart stand still. The long-drawn wail of two old boughs rubbing against each other brought out the perspiration in beads on her forehead. The swoop of bats in the darkness over her was as the wings of unearthly creatures.

118

An aging spruce in the Haunted Wood—
benign by day, able to terrify at night.

With a bit of imagination and a friend to improve on the
stories, all kinds of harrowing things could appear in the
Haunted Wood.

Teeth still chattering with fear, she vows, on her return, to be
content in the future with the ordinary and forgo the imagined
ghastly.

Yet channeled intentionally, their respective imaginations
did much to rescue them from the banal or disappointing, and
whenever it kicks in, the results transform the experience. Such
moments can be as surprising as when Anne is racing to Diana's
house after Minnie May is stricken with a bad case of croup, and
Anne pauses on the way to bask in the romance of the moment.
The passage is typical for its gorgeous writing—"The night was
clear and frosty, all ebony of shadow and silver of snowy slope"—
and for the joy Anne takes from it—how "truly delightful to go
skimming through all this mystery and loveliness with your
bosom friend who has been so long estranged."

119

Sunset over a line of spruce trees, dividing fields not far from Cavendish.

A similar moment occurs when Marilla tells her that Mrs. Barry is poised to apologize to Anne after cutting her off from Diana following the currant wine episode. Anne tears off to the Barrys' to hear the words herself, then she

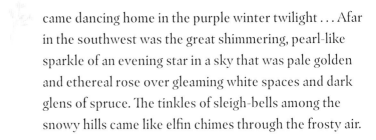

> came dancing home in the purple winter twilight . . . Afar in the southwest was the great shimmering, pearl-like sparkle of an evening star in a sky that was pale golden and ethereal rose over gleaming white spaces and dark glens of spruce. The tinkles of sleigh-bells among the snowy hills came like elfin chimes through the frosty air.

All is right in the world once again, confirmed by the beauty of the natural setting and the graceful sentences that capture it.

120

Equally revealing passages occur often in Montgomery's early journals, many of them notable for their sharply contrasting moments. Almost as soon as Montgomery mentions something grim or unsettling, the writing shifts to a scene so beautiful, so elegantly described, that it's clearly an exercise in restoring the writer's sense of balance and purpose. One such example occurs during the year she spends at the Halifax Ladies College in Nova Scotia; it's Christmas 1895, and she's twenty-one and all alone, as "Grandfather doesn't want to be bothered meeting me or taking me back." She could wallow by herself in her sorrow, or she could pursue what has worked in the past: take a long walk and then pick up her journal, recording all she has seen and sensed when in that heightened state of attention that being outside brought out in her.

On this particular night, the city lies on one side, "its roofs and spires dim in their shroud of violet smoke," while the harbor is off to her right, "taking on tints of rose and coppery gold as it reached out into the sunset." She observes how the "tiny dark headlands cut the creamy expanse, and the opposite shores, softened by the mist, folded into each other in hill and valley of dark and light." The beam from the nearby lighthouse is like a "baleful star" but above it all, in "a concave of stainless blue, where no soil of earth could reach," a half moon shines, "with a maiden veil of pearly vapor drawn chastely over her pure face."

While the passage today sounds a bit hyperbolic, the effect on the author (and thus on the reader) is obvious. The pure face the writer sees in the moon reflects her own earnest attempt to meet it, and in finding the just-right language for that shared moment, she manages to gather all the solace she needs to go on.

Writers of fiction need such an imagination in order to create rich interior lives for their characters, along with believable conflicts that those characters must confront in order to change or grow in some way. Rarely, however, does an author create characters that need to write in order to channel their visions;

121

An open window at Silver Bush provides an invitation to anyone with a passport from the imagination.

they might fire off letters or scribble notes, but these tend to be plot elements, advancing the storyline, rather than something the protagonist is driven to do. Anne Shirley is an exception. Like Maud Montgomery, Anne wants to write, though she downplays her initial attempts, remaining modest about her goals.

It's in the second novel of the Anne series, *Anne of Avonlea* (published in 1909, a year after *Anne of Green Gables*), that we catch a glimpse of Anne writing. Gilbert comes upon her in the act, though she's quick to hide the pages. "I was just trying to write out some of my thoughts . . . but I couldn't get them to please me. They seem so stiff and foolish directly they're written down on white paper with black ink." In *Anne's House of Dreams*, the fourth novel in the series, it's her former student Paul whom Anne sees as having the greater writing talent. "You may be famous yourself, Teacher," he tells her. "I've seen a good deal of your work these last three years." "No," she replies. "I know what I can do. I can write pretty, fanciful little sketches that children love and editors send welcome cheques for. But I can do nothing big. My only chance for earthly immortality is a corner in your Memoirs."

What we do know of Anne is that her goal is to create something beautiful, something memorable, as she says in *Anne of Avonlea*, "I'd like to add some beauty to life." She succeeds in doing that, over the course of the eight novels that tell her story, though it appears through her engagement with the natural world rather than through her literary talents. It won't be until the *Emily*

123

of New Moon trilogy that writing will so possess the main character; Emily *has* to write, which we learn early in the first novel, as
a way to diminish the pain of her circumstances and fully engage
her creativity.

For Maud Montgomery, writing was all those things
and more, as necessary as sleeping or eating, providing her the
moments when she was most alive and happy. Through writing,
she brought together her fertile imagination, her love of beauty,
and her reverence for the natural world. Perhaps nowhere is this
more evident than in a journal entry from May 1900, as she took
stock of the sorrow that had marked the preceding months. In
January of that year, she was delighting in a letter from her father,
whom she corresponded with regularly despite not having seen
him since leaving Saskatchewan. Then, a few days later, came a
telegram announcing his death, "a thunderbolt from a clear sky."
For weeks afterward, she could do little but mourn. "Even when
he was so far away and for so many years, we never grew apart . . .
We always remained near and dear in spirit . . . Oh, what a long,
dreary, dismal winter followed."

After long weeks of silence, she finally finds a way to begin
writing again, word by word, sentence by sentence, until she lifts
herself slowly out of despair. "With the effort came strength and
the old love, inborn and bred, for my pen came back to me." Her
subsequent realization is one of the more poignant moments of

124

I *t was lovely out this evening. I went up over the hill in the clear pure November air and walked about until twilight had deepened into a moonlit autumn night. I was alone but not lonely. Thought was quick and vivid, imagination active and bright. . . . Then I came in, still tingling with the strange, wild, sweet life of the spirit, and wrote a chapter of my new serial—wrote it easily and pleasureably, with no flagging or halting. Oh, it is good to feel well and vivid and interesting and all alive!*

—*THE SELECTED JOURNALS OF L. M. MONTGOMERY*, VOL. 1

the first journal, and could serve as a motto for her life, "Oh, as long as we can work we can make life beautiful."

While both Anne Shirley and Maud Montgomery thrive on meaningful interactions with others and on literature that enriches their souls, they also know that, without the presence of natural beauty, their spirits begin to wither. To ward off such a possibility, as a girl each develops the habit of bringing wild beauty inside, making bouquets of whatever flowers are in season or of boughs and ferns when the blooming time has passed.

126

The hired man's room above the kitchen at Green Gables.

ABOVE LEFT Anne's room at Green Gables, beginning to take on more color after the bareness she first encountered.

As Anne tells Marilla, after gathering maple branches in their full autumn splendor, "one can dream so much better in a room where there are pretty things. I'm going to put these boughs in the old blue jug and set them on my table." Marilla—at least in the novel's beginning—doesn't understand the impulse nor why Anne would see the whitewashed walls of her new bedroom as "so painfully bare and staring that . . . they must ache over their own bareness." Nor does she see that the room "was of a rigidity not to be described in words, but which sent a shiver to the very marrow of Anne's bones."

Anne soon sets about bringing color into the place, each new bouquet yet more evidence of the vitality her presence is

127

adding to the household. Even before she knows for sure that the Cuthberts will keep her, she has arranged a jar of apple blossoms on the dinner table ("Marilla had eyed that decoration askance, but had said nothing"). Such decorations—or the planning and gathering of them—appear again when the minister and his wife come to tea and Anne wants to set a table for them that includes ferns and wild roses. Marilla thinks it's nonsense; in her opinion, "it's the eatables that matter and not flummery decorations." Anne prevails, however, and her arrangement earns praise from the Allans for its artistic loveliness. Unfortunately, the good cheer such beauty enhances doesn't last: the cake Anne had baked was inedible, flavored as it was with anodyne liniment.

Such attention to flower arrangements continues throughout Montgomery's novels, notably in the second book of the series, *Anne of Avonlea*, as when Anne dresses up the table of the

crotchety old neighbor, Mr. Harrison, with a fresh bouquet from
his garden and then "shut her eyes to the stains on the tablecloth";
again when she tries to bolster Marilla's spirits, while they await
word on whether the twins, Dora and Davy, will be claimed by
their uncle, by setting out "a vase of frost-bleached ferns and
ruby-red maple leaves" to brighten the room; and again when
she and Diana prepare an arrangement of yellow dahlias for Miss
Lavendar's wedding, knowing how well it would go with the "dark
background of red hall paper."

Montgomery records similar details in her journals, as
when she's in Belmont on a sleepy April afternoon in 1897, her
hard year at the school almost over. In a vase on the table beside
her, she has placed "a couple of willow sprays thickset with silvery
catkins," which set her to missing the willow tree in the Haunted
Wood and the pussy willows that grew in the front orchard of
her grandparents' home. "How I love trees!" she writes, which
begins a reminiscence of trees she has loved so well "that I would
almost as soon as have one of my fingers cut off as see one of
them cut down—the old birches around the garden, the tall balsam poplars behind the house, the old spruces back of the well
and the cherry trees down the lane." That realization—and her
memory of the paucity of trees at her father's home in Saskatchewan—has her wondering whether she hadn't been "a tree in some
other state of existence." Perhaps, she writes, that is why she has
always had such fondness for trees, and why she feels "so utterly

129

Wallpaper in Green Gables, recreated from original patterns.

Late afternoon sun in billowy Queen Anne's lace, Prince Edward Island.

and *satisfyingly* at home in the woods." The idea of transmigration appeals to her: "It is hard *not* to believe that I have lived somewhere before."

The arc of wondering in the passage, beginning with catkins and ending with possible past life experiences, is not unusual for a writer who begins so many of her scenes with the sensory details that make them come alive. She starts with flowers or landscape colors, then allows her thoughts their fascinating tangents, furnished by all she has seen and recorded from a world seemingly

132

Everything was invested with a kind of fairy grace and charm ... the trees that whispered nightly round the old house where I slept, the woodsy nooks I explored, the homestead fields, each individualized by some oddity of fence or shape, the sea whose murmur was never out of my ears—all were radiant with "the glory and the dream."

—THE ALPINE PATH

narrow—the small villages of Prince Edward Island—yet made far larger by all she has read and remembered.

A close examination of some of the photographs Montgomery took of her rooms in Cavendish reveal the same need that Anne had for bringing the wild world inside, making sure natural beauty was part of the setting before beginning her work. Here the ubiquitous bouquet, there the clutch of autumn leaves, each arranged in a way that suggests they had been placed on the shelf long before Montgomery hauled out her camera to capture the shot.

133

Birches near Green Gables.

An example of Maud Montgomery's bringing the wild inside. Three arrangements with leaves appear in this photo by Montgomery of her room in her grandparents' home in Cavendish, c. 1895.

In another record of Montgomery's personal life—the scrapbooks she created in the 1890s and early 1900s—many of these same elements appear as well, including dried flowers, poems about flowers, flower images cut from catalogs, flowers adorning women's hair, even messages written on neatly cut squares of birch bark. The two earliest scrapbooks, covering the period from 1893 to 1909, can be seen at her birthplace in New London, where they're kept under glass. (They're housed at the Confederation Centre of the Arts, in Charlottetown, during the winter.) The University of Guelph Library in Guelph, Ontario, owns four other scrapbooks and has created a virtual exhibition that includes reproductions of many of the pages and information about some of the items they contain.

135

The inside front cover of Montgomery's *Blue Album*, with images of cut flowers (lilies), strawberries, dried grass, two calendar covers (one with roses and another of a kid glove), and a buckle from the shoe of her Cavendish teacher, Selena Robinson, with "Good luck" written above it and lines from Robert Burns below (Montgomery was about to head off to Prince of Wales College).

Page three of Montgomery's *Blue Album*, with its exuberance of roses and a calling card from her would-be suitor, Mr. Mustard. The object in the middle right is "a scrap of desk" from a Prince of Wales College classroom; "the path of learning is no royal road," she wrote underneath.

This love of wild beauty, so characteristic of both Maud and Anne, has a particularly fascinating effect on the unlikely character of Marilla, who softens more and more with each passing month spent in Anne's company. This trope would be lost on viewers who only know the 1985 movie, starring Megan Follows as Anne and Colleen Dewhurst as Marilla; the film's opening scenes reveal a house already adorned with bouquets, which, while they add color to the set, misrepresent what Anne will come to embody. Other than her lone geranium, Marilla didn't "do" flowers. She didn't grow them; she didn't cut them; she didn't bring them into her house—at least not in the beginning of the novel. It's one of the few things the movie gets wrong.

It's not until after Anne's year at Queen's that Marilla will greet her return by placing a single flowering rose on the

Lucy Maud Montgomery
Blue Album, 1890
Paper scrapbook album
35.5 x 30 x 4 cm
Confederation Centre Art Gallery
CM 67.5.15

Page eighteen of Montgomery's *Blue Album*, with ribbon-tied dried flowers and a Lucy Larcom poem, "The First Song Sparrow." Larcom worked in a cotton mill in Lowell, Massachusetts, from 1835 to 1845 and was part of a self-improvement movement among the mill girls that, among other things, created a literary magazine, *Lowell Offering*. In addition to publishing poems and songs, Larcom went on to teach at the Wheaton Female Seminary, now Wheaton College, served as editor of *Our Young Folks,* and published the memoir *A New England Girlhood.*

windowsill in Anne's bedroom. But after two years of living with Anne's aesthetic impulses, she begins to feel their effect, a slow shift in her outlook and in her openness to the natural world's beauty. One such passage, describing a walk in late April, is so sensuous in its expression that it's hard to believe that Marilla appears in the same sentences.

Marilla is walking home from a church meeting, ostensibly thinking about church matters, when something entirely different begins working its magic on her. She soon becomes aware of "red fields smoking into pale-purply mists in the declining sun, of long sharp-pointed fir shadows falling over the meadow beyond the brook, of still, crimson-budded maples around a mirror-like wood-pool, of a wakening in the world and a stir of hidden pulses under the gray sod." Spring has its smoldering hold on her, and

137

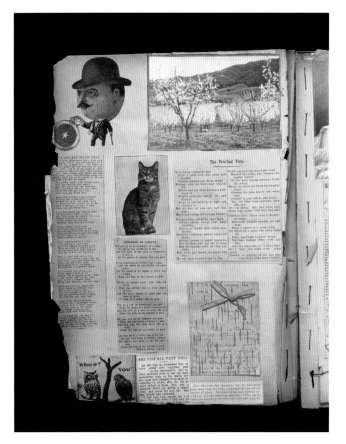

Lucy Maud Montgomery
Red Album, 1890
Paper scrapbook album
38.7 x 28.4 x 4.7 cm
Confederation Centre Art Gallery
CM 67.5.12

Page sixteen of Montgomery's *Red Album*, with a message written on birch bark, a photo of flowering trees, and a poem about ferns.

Anne's influence has left her susceptible to it. As a result, "Marilla's sober, middle-aged step was lighter and swifter because of its deep, primal gladness."

FOR CONTEMPORARY READERS visiting Prince Edward Island, the scope of Maud Montgomery's imagination can make it difficult to figure out what was a "real" site referred to in the novels and what became a composite scene on the page. Maud Montgomery's near photographic memory and her willingness to pull a lake scene from one area, a forest glade from another, and a secret garden from a third (and perhaps a fictional one at that) make it tricky to find Anne's sites when wandering her old haunts. However, for most visitors to Prince Edward Island, this doesn't matter.

The timelessness of the setting—the cliffs and harbors, the brooks and orchards, the church spires as prominent as fir

138

A summer sunset at Cavendish Beach.

An abandoned house and barn at the edge of a Prince Edward Island potato field.

Writing in her journal on October 11, 1889, Montgomery described her love for the woods, and a maple grove in her childhood—"all trees overhead and ferns underfoot."

trees against the horizon—makes Montgomery's descriptions come to life. Pass a stand of tall spruces or pines, their lower limbs dead, their trunks knotted by scars or hairy with lichen, and it's a moment in the Haunted Wood, no matter the location. Or wander a stream where small blossoms of ladies' eardrops lean into the light or ferns rise into a sunbeam from the roots of a tree above a brook, and it's one of the woodland paths that Anne so loved, no matter if it's in Cavendish or mid-island along the Dunk River.

Or listen to the evening sounds in a quiet bay—the lap of waves against a boat hull, the calls of distant gulls, a leaping fish splashing back into the water—and understand what Anne has

The shore near Cavendish, looking out across the Gulf of St. Lawrence.

The ever-changing sky near Cavendish Beach.

in mind when she and Diana are riding back to Avonlea after spending time with Diana's aunt in Charlottetown. Despite enjoying everything the city had to offer, the rural scene exerts an even stronger pull. "Every little cove along the curving road was a marvel of dancing ripples. The waves broke with a soft swish on the rocks below them, and the tang of the sea was in the strong fresh air. 'Oh, but it's good to be alive and to be going home,' breathed Anne." Oh but it's good, one wants to add, that we can still find that home on Prince Edward Island.

143

*I*t is the greatest
pleasure my days
bring to me to go out
to the garden every
morning and see what
new blossoms have
opened overnight.
At such moments my
heart fairly bursts
with gladness.

—THE SELECTED JOURNALS OF
L. M. MONTGOMERY, VOL. 1

EMERALD SCREENS

MAUD'S AND ANNE'S
FAVORITE GARDENS

Maud Montgomery's writings reveal an abiding fondness for three different types of garden: the "old-timey" garden, which she introduced as the Barry garden in *Anne of Green Gables* and which is still known as a grandmother's or old-fashioned garden; the wild garden, which might be a neglected corner or an abandoned plot where hardy perennials delight a wanderer with their unexpected blossoms; and the woodland garden under a canopy of boughs, full of the ephemerals that gave her such delight each spring.

Fair, rich confusion is all the aim of an old-fashioned flower garden, and the greater the confusion, the richer . . . No stiffness, no ceremony—flowers, and not a garden—this is the beauty of the old style.

—ANNA BARTLETT WARNER, AUTHOR OF *GARDENING BY MYSELF*

Bouncing Bet (*Saponaria officinalis*), an old-fashioned plant that Montgomery also called bouncing Bess.

Grandmother's Gardens

When Anne Shirley, still new to the Avonlea community, learns that another girl, Diana Barry, lives nearby, she can hardly contain her excitement. "Oh, Marilla," she says, "I'm frightened . . . What if she shouldn't like me! It would be the most tragical disappointment of my life." Marilla seeks to console her, in her gruff Marilla way, though she can do little to allay the specter of the judgmental Mrs. Barry, who might not take kindly to the queer little orphan.

Yet at the much-anticipated moment when the two girls are finally to meet—and before Montgomery even reveals what they have to say to each other—the author first gives a lengthy description of the garden. It's a fascinating, tantalizing diversion, briefly distracting the reader from the prospects that may or may not await Anne in this "very pretty little girl" with "the merry expression."

For the author, and thus for readers, it clearly matters that, after initial introductions, the two meet outdoors, surrounded by plants—a "bowery wilderness" of them. As they gaze "bashfully at one another over a clump of gorgeous tiger lilies," the reader is likewise invited to bask in the rich array of colors and sounds, the garden's bounty seeming to foreshadow the course of their friendship. We sense how it transports Anne—it takes a moment before she can compose herself enough to whisper her big question to Diana—but at last she's asking Diana if she will like her well

Orange daylily (*Hemerocallis fulva*) at the Anne of Green Gables Historic Site. Anne and Diana meet for the first time amid brightly colored lilies in the Barry garden.

enough to be her bosom friend. The laughing Diana agrees, and repeats the oath to be faithful, a promise that holds true throughout the novel.

Montgomery's tactic, which could have frustrated an impatient reader, pays off. She has reminded us of the importance to Anne of a natural setting, the kind that embodies so much of her emotional and spiritual life and where so many of her significant realizations take place. She has offered a context that allows each girl to be her natural self—innocent, affectionate, joyous—when free of the inside, adult world. And she has given us a way to read the scene that follows—the blossoming of a friendship into something as full of potential as that found in the splendor of the garden.

The Barry garden was a bowery wilderness of flowers which would have delighted Anne's heart at any time less fraught with destiny. It was encircled by huge old willows and tall firs, beneath which flourished flowers that loved the shade. Prim, right-angled paths, neatly bordered with clam-shells, intersected it like moist red ribbons and in the beds between old-fashioned flowers ran riot. There were rosy bleeding-hearts and great splendid crimson peonies; white, fragrant narcissi and thorny, sweet Scotch roses; pink and blue and white columbines and lilac-tinted Bouncing Bets; clumps of southernwood and ribbon grass and mint; purple Adam-and-Eve, daffodils, and masses of sweet clover white with its delicate, fragrant, feathery sprays; scarlet lightning that shot its fiery lances over prim white musk-flowers; a garden it was where sunshine lingered and bees hummed, and winds, beguiled into loitering, purred and rustled.
—ANNE OF GREEN GABLES

There is nothing in the world so sweet as a real "old-timey" garden ... [I]t must be secluded and shut away from the world—a "garden enclosed"—preferably by willows—or apple trees—or firs. It must have some trim walks bordered by clamshells, or edged with "ribbon grass," and there must be in it the flowers that belong to old-fashioned gardens and are seldom found in the catalogues of to-day—perennials planted there by grandmotherly hands when the century was young. There should be poppies, like fine ladies in full-skirted silken gowns, "cabbage" roses, heavy and pink and luscious, tiger-lilies like gorgeously bedight sentinels, "Sweet-William" in striped attire, bleeding-heart, that favorite of my childhood, southernwood, feathery and pungent, butter-and-eggs—that is now known as "narcissus"—"bride's bouquet," as white as a bride's bouquet should be, holly hocks like flaunting overbold maidens, purple spikes of "Adam and Eve," pink and white "musk," "Sweet Balm" and "Sweet May," "Bouncing Bess" in her ruffled, lilac-tinted skirts, pure white "June Lilies," crimson peonies— "pinies"—velvety-eyed "Irish Primroses," which were neither primroses nor Irish, scarlet lightning and Prince's feather—all growing in orderly confusion. Dear old gardens! The very breath of them is a benediction!
—THE SELECTED JOURNALS OF L. M. MONTGOMERY, VOL. 1

Shirley poppies (*Papaver rhoeas*) by a wagon wheel, Avonlea Village, Cavendish, Prince Edward Island.

ABOVE RIGHT Double bouncing Bet or soapwort (*Saponaria officinalis* 'Flore Pleno')

That the Barry garden is so similar to Maud Montgomery's ideal flower garden—the passages from the novel echo the descriptions in Montgomery's journal—is another reminder of the sensibilities that Maud and Anne share, as well as what each believed that gardens should reveal of their owners. Gardens, they felt, should display a distinct aesthetic, an extension of one's idea of beauty, a place of sensory pleasures. By "garden," Montgomery typically means a flower garden. As the title character of *The Story Girl* (1911) makes clear, "Oh, I never like the vegetable garden . . . Except when I am hungry. Then I *do* like to go and look at the nice little rows of onions and beets. But I love a flower garden. I think I could be always good if I lived in a garden all the time."

Staking out such a preference for the old-timey garden put Maud Montgomery at odds with those who welcomed the annual push toward the new and exotic. Then, as now, seed catalogs arrived in winter, when the craving for flowers and colors was its most acute, the pages full of endless possibilities for transforming

Anne Shirley calls the fruit of *Rosa rugosa* "roseberries," and she and Diana make necklaces of them.

a front or back yard. Ranging in size from a modest few dozen pages to an exuberant two hundred, the late-nineteenth-century catalogs were arranged much as they are today. The newest varieties appeared in the opening pages, followed by vegetables, flowers, lawn seeds, and farmers' needs (such as grains and seed corn), all in alphabetical order; the larger companies might also include climbing vines, bulbs, or berries. While the smaller suppliers typically had but a few illustrations, limiting themselves to lists of plants and their prices, the bigger companies used color lithographs for the front and back covers, detailed black-and-white drawings of select varieties scattered throughout, along with an occasional full-page painting; by the early twentieth century, photographs began to supplement the lengthy descriptions.

BELOW RIGHT Front cover of Farquhar's 1902 catalog, with an image of hollyhocks that look almost like peonies in their number of petals.

Front cover from a 1902 John Lewis Childs catalog, featuring "New, Giant Flowered Geraniums."

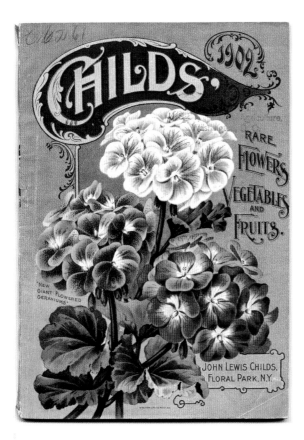

From the very first page, the enticements beckoned. From unexpected colors to an over-the-top doubling in size or number of petals (peonies, asters, daffodils), the latest fashions made big splashes, and the catalogs displayed them to their best advantage.

Montgomery didn't appear to be seduced—flowers in her old-timey garden were "seldom found in the catalogues" of the day—which aligned her with the type of literature she had immersed herself in for years as well as with the burgeoning Arts and Crafts movement. She knew by heart whole poems by Whittier, Longfellow, Tennyson, Burns—nature-based writers whose values and vocabularies became or meshed with her own. They eschewed the built life and trappings of the Industrial Age, seeking instead the visceral and the ineffable that could be found only in the natural world. Likewise, adherents of the relatively new Arts and Crafts movement sought a return to work that was handmade, the one-of-a-kind tool or piece of furniture, the elegantly crafted thing that bore its own unique story. When Montgomery claimed that the ideal garden, like the poet, must "be born not made . . . The least flavor of newness or modernity spoils it," she was allying herself with a position that critics and art lovers around the world were beginning to advance.

We learn, after his sudden death in *Anne of Green Gables*, that Matthew Cuthbert shared a similar fondness for old-timey flowers. At the funeral, there were flowers all around his

Simple, old-fashioned hollyhocks (*Alcea rosea*), Cavendish, Prince Edward Island.

155

Imperial Japanese
MORNING GLORY

THE HANDSOMEST CLIMBER IN CULTIVATION.
PRICE PER PACKET, SINGLE & DOUBLE MIXED. 6 CTS.

MISS C·H·LIPPINCOTT, 319 & 323 SIXTH ST. S. MINNEAPOLIS, MINN.

One of the first women to start her own seed company, Miss C. H. Lippincott highlights the influence of foreign markets—and the Japanese aesthetic, in particular—in this back cover image for her 1897 catalog, "Imperial Japanese Morning Glory: The Handsomest Climber in Cultivation."

coffin—"sweet old-fashioned flowers which his mother had planted in the homestead garden in her bridal days and for which Matthew had always had a secret wordless love." Later, when Anne chooses a bush to plant on his grave, it, too, is of the old-fashioned kind—a white Scotch rose descended from one that his mother had carried over from Scotland.

Similar descriptions of flowering plants appear in the short story "A Garden of Old Delights" (1910), which Montgomery later integrated into the beginning section of *The Story Girl*; ironically it's the garden of an actual grandmother that forms the story's setting, her loving nurture of each of the flower beds essential to their emotional impact. (Montgomery's own grandmother, who forbore anything that might be seen as frivolous or impractical, never appears in her granddaughter's writings as either laboring in or caring about a flower garden.)

In appearance, a grandmother's garden resisted excess, startling color, and blooms so heavy their stalks needed support. Miss Lavendar, for example, won't have dahlias in her garden in *Anne of Avonlea*; "she did not like them and they would not have suited the fine retirement of her old-fashioned garden." To be true to its aesthetic, such a garden also resisted the formality of a typical Victorian layout, opting instead for a more natural look—"orderly confusion," Montgomery called it—which appealed to those like Maud and Anne, with their shared value of intimacy with the natural world and a means of entering it without artifice.

Carnations (*Dianthus caryophyllus*) on the cover of E. J. Bowen's Catalogue of 1902, in a color and size that wouldn't have appeared in a grandmother's garden; most dianthus are pale to dark pink (hence another common name—pinks).

Given Montgomery's literary tastes and her fondness for native plants and trees, which she often personified as friends (as Anne says to Diana in *Anne of Avonlea*: "That white birch you caught me kissing is a sister of mine. The only difference is, she's a tree and I'm a girl, but that's no real difference"), it followed that she would advocate a style of gardening that emphasized natural settings and traditional species, including those native to the area as well as those that the first settlers to the region brought over. In her writings, she doesn't dwell on such garden features as height or texture or accent colors, but fragrance is paramount, as is the perceived sense of wildness and organic naturalness—shrubs integrated with flowers, fruit trees on the periphery, paths that follow the contours of the land instead of adhering to artificial, linear schemes. To an untrained eye such gardens could appear reckless and messy; yet to the trained observer, the scene reassured,

157

Trumpet honeysuckle (*Lonicera sempervirens*)

and the visitor knew that, in the designer of the garden, she had met a like-minded soul.

When writing about her personal life, however, Montgomery rarely describes the labor required to maintain the ideal garden. In the essay she wrote about her career, *The Alpine Path*, she treats the gardens she worked hard to create with Well and Dave (the two boys boarded with her grandparents for three years when she was a girl) in a very lighthearted way. "Our carrots and parsnips, our lettuces and beets, our phlox and sweet-peas—either failed to come up at all, or dragged a pallid, spindling existence to an ignoble end, in spite of all our patient digging, manuring, weeding, and watering, or, perhaps, because of it, for I fear we were more zealous than wise." The one bright spot? "[A] few hardy sunflowers which, sown in an uncared-for spot, throve better than all our petted darlings, and lighted up a corner of the spruce grove with their cheery golden lamps."

Similarly, her journals include but a few references to the act of gardening itself, the most notable appearing in 1905, when she was beginning work on *Anne of Green Gables*. With the warming weather of spring, she was able to move back upstairs to her preferred room, which she had to vacate each fall as her grandmother refused to heat it during the winter. The effect on her emotional wellbeing was profound and immediate, a seasonal

158

difference "between happiness and unhappiness." Milder days also meant the chance to attend to a second love: "I almost live up there [in the room]—what time I don't live in my garden." She wrote and she gardened, the two creative acts reinforcing each other as she labored on the threshold of fame.

My garden—oh, the delight it has been to me this summer! I am positively reveling in flowers. Roses—such roses! My big bush of blush doubles, which never did anything before, flung all its hoarded sweetness of three years into bloom— dozens of the most lovely blossoms. There is a big vaseful on my tables before me now. And behind me are other vases full of the sweetest of sweet peas and yellow poppies, and nasturtiums like breaths of flame . . . Oh, what a wise old myth it was that placed the creation of life in a garden.

BELOW LEFT Hollyhocks against a porch railing, with *Delphinium* hybrids in the back and poppy pods and daylilies in the foreground.

Orange and yellow nasturtiums in the foreground; purple *Liatris spicata*, also known as blazing star or gayfeather in the middle; and several varieties of daylilies in the background. Cavendish, Prince Edward Island.

Peony, a favorite perennial; Montgomery referred to
peonies as "pinies" in her description of the ideal garden.

Maud Montgomery's garden in Leaskdale, Ontario, with its flower-covered arch. Photograph by L. M. Montgomery, c. 1917.

Additional garden descriptions don't appear in her journals until after her marriage to Ewan Macdonald, in 1911, when they moved to Leaskdale, Ontario, and she could finally design the kind of garden she had long wanted. "We have been gardening furiously since housecleaning was finished," she writes, "and I am besottedly happy in it . . . I had to go without one for so many years and now I'm quite drunk with the joy of having one again." At another point, she refers to the destruction of her garden by a sudden cloudburst, when "a perfect river rushed down the hill and swept our garden out of existence in a twinkling—the garden I had worked so hard to get in, doing all the digging and preparing myself." More typical in her journal entries from the Ontario years is the occasional mention of the canning she has done, the preserves she has just put up—pears, plums, cherries, raspberries—listed as briefly as when she summarizes other household chores.

The reasons may be many for this lack of attention to gardens in her journals: a natural resistance to mentioning chores or physical labor (Anne Shirley doesn't dwell on such things either), a disappointment when her gardens couldn't meet her high expectations, or such a commitment to the most important work of her

161

A view of the back garden from the kitchen window, Leaskdale, Ontario. Photograph by L. M. Montgomery, c. 1917.

life—her writing—that gardens, much as they soothed, had to fall away. Where Montgomery seemed happiest was in creating gardens on the page, conjuring them visually by listing the species of flowers, much as she did in *Anne of Green Gables* with the Barry garden. In *Anne of the Island*, she adds a variety of annuals to a garden "sweet with dear, old fashioned, unworldly flowers and shrubs—sweet may, southernwood, lemon verbena, alyssum, petunias, marigolds and chrysanthemums." And in "A Garden of Old Delights," she names the flowers in the main garden—peonies, hollyhocks, lilies, clove-pinks, narcissus, and roses (old and sturdy enough, she writes, that they were never bothered by mildew or insect pests), and then turns her attention to the "very old-fashioned bed full of bleeding hearts, Sweet William, bride's bouquet, butter-and-eggs, Adam-and-Eve, columbines, pink and white daisies, and Bouncing Bets." As with so many local names for plants, the identity of Montgomery's purple-spiked Adam-and-Eve remains a mystery.

162

Maud Montgomery's son Chester, as a toddler in their garden in Leaskdale, Ontario.
Photograph by L. M. Montgomery, c. 1914.

Pale hollyhocks and daylilies at Green Gables.

Montgomery's archives yield but one photograph of a Prince Edward Island garden that she might consider ideal—"old Mrs. George Macneill's garden," the likely inspiration for the Barry garden, with vines climbing the walls and flowers spilling into the central pathway.

Alma Macneill and her mother at the site of the garden in Cavendish that likely inspired the Barry garden in *Anne of Green Gables*. Montgomery referred to it as "old Mrs. George Macneill's garden." Photograph by L. M. Montgomery, c. 1897.

165

Past the spruces the lane dipped down into a sunny little open where a log bridge spanned a brook; and then came the glory of a sunlit beechwood where the air was like transparent golden wine, and the leaves fresh and green, and the wood floor a mosaic of tremulous sunshine. Then more wild cherries, and a little valley of lissome firs, and then a hill so steep that the girls lost their breath climbing it; but when they reached the top and came out into the open the prettiest surprise of all awaited them.

—*ANNE OF AVONLEA*

In late summer, pink spires of fireweed (*Chamerion angustifolium*), which can grow as tall as eight feet, appear along fields and recently disturbed edges.

Wild Gardens

Helter-skelter is not an easy appearance to cultivate; it takes considerable care to make a garden look as though it sprang up naturally, reckless and exuberant in its very wildness. Perhaps that's why Montgomery found neglected or forest gardens so attractive, shaped as they were by the forces of nature. In "A Garden of Old Delights," the unnamed narrator loves the wild garden the best, "a sunny triangle shut in by the meadow fences and as full of wild flowers as it could hold: blue and white violets, dandelions, Junebells, wild-roses, daisies, buttercups, asters, and goldenrod, all lavish in their season." In *Kilmeny of the Orchard* (1910), an abandoned orchard provides the idyllic setting for the relationship between the mute Kilmeny and the new teacher, Eric, that will result in her regaining her power of speech and his learning to love the Prince Edward Island setting that had originally seemed so pastoral that he wasn't sure he could tolerate a month on its shores. The setting made all the difference.

 Most of the orchard was grown over lushly with grass; but at the end where Eric stood there was a square, treeless place which had evidently once served as a homestead garden. Old paths were still visible, bordered by stones and large pebbles. There were two clumps of lilac trees; one blossoming in royal purple, the other in white.

167

Rosa rugosa, double form. Green Gables, Cavendish, Prince Edward Island.

ABOVE RIGHT Phlox (*Phlox paniculata*) was a favorite of many early gardeners; its presence in an overgrown area often indicates an abandoned homestead.

Between them was a bed ablow with the starry spikes of June lilies. Their penetrating, haunting fragrance distilled on the dewy air in every soft puff of wind. Along the fence rosebushes grew, but it was as yet too early in the season for roses.

Beyond was the orchard proper, three long rows of trees with green avenues between, each tree standing in a wonderful blow of pink and white.

The charm of the place took sudden possession of Eric as nothing had ever done before.

In *Anne of Avonlea*, Hester Gray's abandoned garden—and the romantic and tragic story that accompanies it—deeply affects Anne and her friends when they discover it while setting off on a spring picnic. From its location between beeches and firs, to its

168

moss-covered stone walls and border of blossoming cherry trees, everything about the small plot entrances them. Most compelling of all are the naturalized flowers—the spring bulbs that continued to multiply, year after year. "There were traces of old paths still and a double line of rosebushes through the middle; but all the rest of the space was a sheet of yellow and white narcissi, in their airiest, most lavish, wind-swayed bloom above the lush green grasses."

The girls—Anne, Jane, and Priscilla—listen raptly as Diana tells the story of Hester's husband's devotion; as Hester became increasingly ill, he carried her daily to the garden, until the day she was dying, when "he picked all the roses that were out and heaped

Clematis, a popular climbing plant for trellises, fences, and porch posts.

them over her; and she just smiled up at him . . . and closed her eyes . . . and that . . . was the end."

To die so loved and in a garden! The effect may have been especially acute on Anne, who, when the girls eventually settle down for their picnic, suddenly startles them by pointing at the brook and exclaiming, "Look, do you see that poem?"

"Where?" Jane and Diana stared, as if expecting to see Runic rhymes on the birch trees.

"There . . . down in the brook . . . that old green, mossy log with the water flowing over it in those smooth ripples that look as if they'd been combed, and that single shaft of sunshine falling right athwart it, far down into the pool. Oh, it's the most beautiful poem I ever saw."

Jane finally decides it's more of a picture than a poem. But not so to Anne, to whom "The lines and verses are only the outward garments of the poem . . . The real poem is the soul within them . . . and that beautiful bit is the soul of an unwritten poem."

Though a classic case of beauty residing in the beholder's eyes, it's also a continuation of the trope of wild elegance that the

170

sheer abundance of narcissi set in motion. To one so inclined, a grand drift of white blooms floating above a carpet of lush grass invites finding similar scenes in the surrounding world, the ordinary made extraordinary through a shift in the light, a different means of approach, a willingness simply to be present and pay attention.

The graceful shapes of aging fruit trees.

171

It was a little narrow, twisting path, winding down over a long hill straight through Mr. Bell's woods, where the light came down sifted through so many emerald screens that it was as flawless as the heart of a diamond. It was fringed in all its length with slim young birches, white-stemmed and lissom boughed; ferns and starflowers and wild lilies-of-the-valley and scarlet tufts of pigeon berries grew thickly along it; and always there was a delightful spiciness in the air and music of bird calls and the murmur and laugh of wood winds in the trees overhead.

—ANNE OF GREEN GABLES

Birches and spruce trees beginning to form a canopy over a narrow dirt road.

Woodland Gardens

No other forest smells as spicy as the boreal forest; no flowers are as hardy and as delicate as those that open under a stand of spruce and fir in spring; and no other woods embody the same kind of spiritual home than the one that Maud and Anne found under the conifers' cathedral-like spires. This northern forest, consisting of various species of spruce, fir, birch, and larch, dominates the Prince Edward Island landscape and inspired some of Maud Montgomery's most rapturous passages.

To Anne Shirley, one species of these trees—the firs—are stately, they're friendly, and "there is no sweeter music on earth than that which the wind makes in the fir-trees at evening." When a fir tree is cut into, Anne is convinced that the "delicious aroma" must indicate their very souls. And on the bitterest of nights, when the moonlight reflected off the snow is glaringly bright, and there is "no soft blending, or kind obscurity, or elusive mistiness in that searching glitter," Anne realizes that "the only things that held their own individuality were the

173

Crested wood fern
(*Dryopteris cristata*)

To Anne, twinflowers (*Linnaea borealis*) are the "shyest and sweetest of woodland blooms."

firs—for the fir is the tree of mystery and shadow, and yields never to the encroachments of crude radiance."

These favorite trees of both Anne and Maud are part of a boreal forest that stretches across most of Canada and appears at high elevations in the continental United States and across the northernmost reaches of Europe and Asia. In these dark-hued woods, mosses and ferns abound and streams keep the shaded areas verdant and moist. Dense evergreen boughs make everything below them feel lush and well protected. When Montgomery designed a questionnaire for herself, modeled on one she had just read, her answer to the question "favorite object in Nature?" was the straightforward "A Prince Edward Island wood of fir and maple, where the ground is carpeted thick with ferns." (She then

174

Anne sees starflowers (*Lysimachia borealis*) as "like the spirits of last year's blossoms."

shifts her reply to something even more specific: "my favorite object in Nature is *Lover's Lane*.")

The first blossoms to appear in the understory in spring—twinflower, starflower, Canada dogwood (also known as bunchberry or crackerberry), and Canada mayflower (wild lily of the valley)—look almost too delicate when snow might still fall and temperatures drop well below freezing. Their slender pale blooms belie their hardiness, however, and account for their presence throughout *Anne of Green Gables*, creating another kind of flowerbed that Anne and Maud relish.

The ferns and flowers that Anne and Diana find in their favorite places—Willowmere, the Dryad's Bubble, Violet Vale, and the Haunted Wood—matter as much to the story as do those

175

Canada dogwood or bunchberry (*Cornus canadensis*) in bloom.

The fruit of Canada dogwood; Anne also calls them pigeon berries, a term perhaps derived from what John Stewart in his *Account Of Prince Edward Island* (1806) noted was their ability to "fatten fowl fast."

Canada mayflower or wild lily of the valley (*Maianthemum canadense*), also referred to as rice lilies in *Anne of Green Gables*.

Red-berried elder (*Sambucus pubens*)

planted by the hands of a gardener or wood fairy, whether setting them out in spring or banking them under a cover of mulch for winter. As Anne tells Marilla after an outing to the Haunted Wood, "All the little wood things—the ferns and the satin leaves and the crackerberries—have gone to sleep, just as if somebody had tucked them away until spring under a blanket of leaves. I think it was a little gray fairy with a rainbow scarf that came tiptoeing along the last moonlight night and did it."

Here, under a tree canopy, is the original garden, the place where Anne imagines being wed, much to the chagrin of Marilla and Rachel Lynde, who believe it would be terribly queer and maybe even illegal to be married outside. For Anne, however, the ideal setting would be "a June dawn, with a glorious sunrise, and roses blooming in the gardens; and I would slip down and meet Gilbert and we would go together to the heart of the beech woods—and there, under the green arches that would be like a splendid cathedral, we would be married."

After her marriage to Ewan (a traditional wedding, in the parlor at Park Corner), Maud Montgomery moved far from the woodland gardens of her childhood, taking pleasure instead in the gardens in Leaskdale, where they lived from 1911 to 1926, and later in Norval, Ontario, where they stayed for the next nine years. Many Anne fans wondered whether, after Ewan retired from the ministry in 1935, Maud might move back to Prince Edward Island; she had, after all, admitted after one visit, "Oh, I felt that

177

Sunlit ferns, ever-present in the understory.

Maud Montgomery in her garden in Norval, Ontario, 1932.

Even the roadsides radiate the fullness of summer in the hum of insects and the drift of flowers.

I belonged there—that I had done some violence to my soul when I left it." Prince Edward Island was the landscape she most loved, the setting she used for all but one of her novels, the blueprint in her mind for an idyllic life.

She settled instead on simply carrying it with her—an island made timeless by its location; its reliance on fishing and farming, which kept its visual landscape relatively unchanged; and its very hold on her imagination, which was peopled with a large community of fictional characters by then. In romanticizing

179

and fabricating aspects of the land, she made it possible for generations of readers to do the same. Her return visits reinforced her vision of the place, but she didn't seem to need to live there again to keep all the old memories alive.

In her homes in Leaskdale and Norval, Ontario, she had family and friends, and literary connections and status, all of which provided myriad reasons to stay. A series of domestic troubles meant she couldn't resettle the household far from a network of help and support, and the ongoing and expensive legal battle with her original publisher meant she had to maintain her same writing pace, even as a busy wife and mother of two sons, in order to help meet the family's financial obligations. Perhaps, too, once she had worked the soil around each new home, finding a way to love each location, she established the necessary relationship with place that only a gardener can truly know.

"I love my garden," Anne Shirley Blythe says in *Anne's House of Dreams*, "and I love working in it. To potter with green, growing things, watching each day to see the dear, new sprouts come up, is like taking a hand in creation, I think. Just now my garden is like faith—the substance of things hoped for." As in so many instances, her words sound like the heartfelt belief of her kindred spirit, Maud Montgomery.

Maud Montgomery in a field of daisies, Prince Edward Island, c. 1935.

$\mathcal{S}$pring is the best time to walk in the woods; at least, we think so in spring; but when summer comes it seems better still; and autumn woods are things quite incomparable in their splendor; and sometimes the winter woods, with their white reserve and fearlessly displayed nakedness, seem the rarest and finest of all. For it is with the forest as with a sweetheart of flesh and blood, in every changing mood and vesture she is still more adorable in her beloved's eyes.

—"SPRING IN THE WOODS," *THE CANADIAN MAGAZINE*, MAY 1911

A WORLD WITH OCTOBERS

THE SEASONS OF
PRINCE EDWARD ISLAND

ost visitors to Prince Edward Island arrive in the summer, a season marked primarily by long hours of sunlight, mild temperatures, and gentle breezes. The island is far enough north to have nearly sixteen hours of daylight by mid-June (three-quarters of an hour longer than New York, and more than an hour longer than San Francisco or Tokyo), while daytime temperatures in July and August average in the mid-70s F. The beaches invite swimmers, the Confederation Trail bikers, and the markets and festivals brim with good cheer.

Yet summer represents only a small part of Anne's and Maud's worlds, engaged as each is in noticing subtle changes in the natural world year-round. Anne gives us frequent glimpses of the different seasons in *Anne of Green Gables*, waxing poetic no matter the weather, while Maud Montgomery, in her journals, provides frequent evidence of the sustenance she derives from the changing landscape as well as the effect on her soul when the weather is so stormy and cold that she is unable to get outside and be replenished in the places she loves. But such blue periods, as Montgomery calls them, are relatively few. The prevailing theme throughout both the novel and Montgomery's Cavendish journals is that the outside world is a glorious place, with every season bringing forth new hues, new sights, and new reminders of the beauty of Prince Edward Island.

186

The wind across a field of ripening wheat (seen here on Prince Edward Island) can make it look like moving water, an extension of the sea just beyond.

Spring had come once more to Green Gables—the beautiful, capricious, reluctant Canadian spring, lingering along through April and May in a succession of sweet, fresh, chilly days, with pink sunsets and miracles of resurrection and growth.

—ANNE OF GREEN GABLES

An early spring view of Green Gables, from the bridge on the trail to the Haunted Wood.

Spring

Spring—the season of tiny pale mayflowers, or, as Montgomery describes them, "the initials of spring's first lettering . . . that have in them the very soul of all the springs that ever were"; their much-anticipated arrival sets in motion Anne's mayflower picnic in Avonlea and Maud's in Cavendish. Spring is also the time of violets, particularly those grown as thickly as in Violet Vale, "all the grass enskied with them," along with great drifts of narcissus that Rachel Lynde lets Anne gather by the armful after apologizing (at Matthew's urging) for behaving so terribly when the two first met.

Spring is when twinflowers first appear in the woods—"those shyest and sweetest of woodland blooms"—and the "pale, aerial starflowers, like the spirits of last year's blossoms." And in her journal, spring is the season that Montgomery will choose, in answering the question as to which is her favorite, with an exclamation point for added emphasis. "Spring—spring—spring! The last two weeks of May in Ontario, the first two of June in P.E. Island. Who could love any

189

Early speedwell (*Veronica persica*)

Perennial cornflower (*Centaurea montana*)

OPPOSITE After Anne apologized, Mrs. Lynde encouraged her to "pick a bouquet of them white June lilies, over in the corner if you like." Narcissus (Montgomery was careful to use the formal "narcissi" for the plural) shows up often in the novels, a perennial favorite of Anne Shirley.

191

Recently plowed fields,
ready for the first
planting of spring.

season better than spring?" "Spring in the Woods" appears as the
first of four essays about the seasons that she'll write in 1911 for
The Canadian Magazine, and reveals the way she approaches the
forested landscape.

> Believe me, it is of no use to seek the woods from any
> motive except sheer love of them; they will find us out at
> once and hide all their sweet, world-old secrets from us.
> But if they know we come to them because we love them
> they will be very kind to us . . . for the woods when they
> give at all give unstintedly.

192

Early lupines, now a ubiquitous flower on the island, add dramatic color to the roadsides.

Spring, too, is when Anne and Matthew take their last walk together, though neither could know they wouldn't have another chance, as he was to die the next day.

She never forgot that day; it was so bright and golden and fair, so free from shadow and so lavish of blossom. Anne spent some of its rich hours in the orchard; she went to the Dryad's Bubble and Willowmere and Violet Vale . . . and finally in the evening she went with Matthew for the cows, through Lovers' Lane to the back pasture. The woods were all gloried through with sunset and the warm splendour of it streamed through the hill gaps in the west.

193

Flowering apple tree, Park Corner. Photograph by L. M. Montgomery, c. 1890s.

An apple tree just
beginning to blossom.

The two talk about his weariness, and Anne's guilt that she wasn't
the boy that he and Marilla had wanted, someone who could have
relieved him of some of the hard work of the farm. But he wouldn't
have taken a dozen boys, he tells her, over the chance to have had
her. And it wasn't a boy, was it, he says, who had just won the cov-
eted Avery scholarship. "It was a girl," he says, "my girl—my girl
that I'm proud of."

195

The spring woods are all spiritual. They charm us through the senses of eye and ear—delicate tintings and aerial sounds, like a maiden's dreams set to music. But the summer woods make a more sensuous appeal.

—"THE WOODS IN SUMMER," THE CANADIAN MAGAZINE, SEPT. 1911

A field of clover near Charlottetown,
Prince Edward Island.

Summer

Summer on Prince Edward Island begins in mid-June, when the daytime temperatures average 67°F and the land has turned lush and green again. For the Avonlea children, liberated from school, summer meant leisurely hours spent boating and picnicking, trouting and berrying ("Who that has eaten strawberries, grass-new from the sunny corners of summer woods, can ever forget them?"). When the doctor advises Marilla to keep "that red-headed girl of yours in the open air all summer and don't let her read books until she gets more spring in her step," striking fear in her about the threat of consumption, Anne has "the golden summer of her life . . . She walked, rowed, berried and dreamed to her heart's content."

On an evening in August, when fireflies blinked through the fields and the cooling air brought out the woods' smells, Anne came "dancing up the lane, like a wind-blown sprite." Though her excitement stems from the invitation she has just received to tea at the Allans', she seems also to be riding the very joy of a summer night. She radiates a similar spirit after the tea party, when "she came home through the twilight, under a great, high-sprung sky gloried over with trails of saffron and rosy cloud, in a beatified state of mind." While she describes the evening to Marilla, the author reminds us of the setting.

197

*H*aying began today, which means that the best half of the summer is over. And now the field before my window is a sweep of silvery swaths gleaming in the hot afternoon sun and the wind that is rustling in the poplars is bringing up whiffs of the fragrance of ripening grasses.

—*THE SELECTED JOURNALS OF L. M. MONTGOMERY, VOL. 1*

Macneill relatives with a wagonload of hay, Cavendish. Photograph by L. M. Montgomery, c. 1920.

Cows in a summer pasture, Prince Edward Island. Photograph by L. M. Montgomery, c. 1890s.

Lilacs in blossom, Park Corner.
Photograph by L. M. Montgomery, c. 1890s.

A profusion of lilac
blooms in June.

A cool wind was blowing down over the long harvest
fields from the rims of firry western hills and whistling
through the poplars. One clear star hung above the
orchard and the fireflies were flitting over in Lovers' Lane,
in and out among the ferns and rustling boughs. Anne
watched them as she talked and somehow felt that wind
and stars and fireflies were all tangled up together into
something unutterably sweet and enchanting.

201

An early summer view from the Lucy Maud Montgomery Land Trust Trail, to the west of Cavendish Beach.

It's an entanglement that would seem less so without Anne in its midst, her vitality as much a part of the landscape as that of every other living being that inhabits it.

As a girl, Maud Montgomery shared many of the same summer activities as Anne, while also spending considerable time at the nearby shore. During vacations, as she writes in *The Alpine Path*, the children would often be pressed into service to deliver lunch to the men fishing for mackerel, and would then stay for the rest of the day at the beach. "I soon came to know every cove, headland, and rock on that shore. We would watch the boats through the sky-glass, paddle in the water, gather shells and pebbles and mussels, and sit on the rocks and eat dulse [a type of edible seaweed], literally, by the yard."

She writes, too, of finding large white shells, "as big as our fists, that had been washed ashore from some distant strand or

202

deep sea haunt." With the words from Oliver Wendell Holmes's "The Chambered Nautilus" in mind, she imagines herself "sitting dreamily on a big boulder with my bare, wet feet tucked up under my print skirt, holding a huge 'snail' shell in my sunburned paw and appealing to my soul 'to build thee more stately mansions.'" It's easy to imagine Anne, barefooted and sun-kissed (or maybe more freckled), taking a similar flight of fancy with a treasure tossed up by the sea.

BELOW LEFT Cavendish Beach in the summer.

BELOW RIGHT Long rows of corn curve with the contours of the land.

Maud Montgomery's photograph shows the Campbell family, including Aunt Annie and Uncle John, along the north shore of Prince Edward Island, c. 1890s. This famous landmark was known as Teapot Rock in Montgomery's time, but the back "handle" has since eroded away, so locals have renamed it Teacup Rock.

October was a beautiful month at Green Gables, when the birches in the hollow turned as golden as sunshine and the maples behind the orchard were royal crimson and the wild cherry-trees along the lane put on the loveliest shades of dark red and bronzy green, while the fields sunned themselves in aftermaths. . . . "Oh, Marilla," [Anne] exclaimed one Saturday morning, coming dancing in with her arms full of gorgeous boughs, "I'm so glad I live in a world where there are Octobers."

—ANNE OF GREEN GABLES

Autumn leaves beginning to turn color on the island.

Fall

Autumn comes fairly quickly to the island, marked most visibly by the end of the tourist season and the changing colors of the trees, a brilliant display that typically lasts throughout the month of October. By early September, the lupines have all gone by, though goldenrods and asters still bloom along the roadsides. The last hay has been baled, the apple trees are heavy with fruit, and the ocean begins to appear more moody and dark. Night begins arriving noticeably earlier than in July, especially in the woods, and as Anne brings the cows home down Lover's Lane one September evening, she sees "All the gaps and clearings . . . brimmed up with ruby sunset light. Here and there the lane was splashed with it, but for the most part it was already quite shadowy beneath the maples, and the spaces under the firs were filled with a clear violet dusk like airy wine."

She's deep into the world of a Sir Walter Scott poem when she comes upon Diana, who's full of news to share, and Anne greets her with a description that seems to have absorbed

207

Cattails, also known as bulrushes (*Typha* species), in late autumn light; the seed heads begin to disintegrate in the fall, their cottony fluff blown about by the wind.

autumn's very hues. "Isn't this evening just like a purple dream, Diana? It makes me so glad to be alive. In the mornings I always think the mornings are best; but when evening comes I think it's lovelier still."

Autumns were a bit tougher for the young Maud, after she leaves the Cavendish school and begins to make her way in the world, the season stunning in its splendor but bittersweet in what it came to represent. With autumn came the start of new teaching positions, and long, often lonely hours by herself that coincided with a slow fading of the light and fewer hours to wander outside. While still in Lower Bedeque and just shy of her twenty-fourth birthday, she writes: "Harvest is ended and summer is gone."

208

Autumn leaves beginning to carpet the ground.

Some of the many different colors of autumn on Prince Edward Island—the reds and golds of maple and birch on one side and the dark green of spruce and fir on the other.

It is October and autumn. We are having delightful fall days, misty and purple, with a pungent, mellow air and magnificent sunsets, followed by the rarest of golden twilights and moonlit nights floating in silver. Maple and birch are crimson and gold and the fields sun themselves in aftermaths. But it is autumn and[,] beautiful as everything is[,] it is the beauty of decay—the sorrowful beauty of the end.

Despite the initial upbeat tenor of the entry, with its celebration of the season's colors, the writing begins to turn, even as autumn does, for her next lines describe her emotional state as neither happy nor at peace. Unlike Anne, who might be sitting near Marilla in a warm firelit room—"curled up Turk-fashion on the hearthrug, gazing into that joyous glow where the sunshine of a hundred summers was being distilled from the maple cord-wood"—Maud was beginning to experience "the infinite sadness of living," and autumn was the time when its ache became most acute.

211

It had been a very mild December and people had looked forward to a green Christmas; but just enough snow fell softly in the night to transfigure Avonlea. Anne peeped out from her frosted gable window with delighted eyes. The firs in the Haunted Wood were all feathery and wonderful; the birches and wild cherry-trees were outlined in pearl; the ploughed fields were stretches of snowy dimples; and there was a crisp tang in the air that was glorious.

—ANNE OF GREEN GABLES

Late afternoon on the island, where the sun sets early in winter.

Winter

Winter is the season when, as Maud Montgomery writes, "people like to cuddle down and count their mercies." From November to April, the island receives an average of ten feet of snow, while temperatures typically range from 10 to 26°F. Bitter winds can make it feel much colder, while calm, crystalline days can transform the outer world, often sending both Maud and Anne into blissful or exuberant moments, seemingly impervious to the harsh weather. On one such winter day, after rescuing Minnie May from her terrible bout with croup, Anne wanders home

in the wonderful, white-frosted winter morning, heavy-eyed from loss of sleep, but still talking unweariedly to Matthew as they crossed the long white field and walked under the glittering fairy arch of the Lover's Lane maples. "Oh, Matthew, isn't it a wonderful morning? The world looks like something God had just imagined for His own pleasure, doesn't it? . . . I'm so glad I live in a world where there are white frosts, aren't you?"

213

Heavy frost on the sand dunes near the Panmure Island Lighthouse, on the eastern shore of Prince Edward Island.

The night of the first concert that Anne attends (and where she feigns disinterest in Gilbert's recitation) is made even more memorable by the sleigh ride she and Diana take to get there.

Anne revelled in the drive to the hall, slipping along over the satin-smooth roads with the snow crisping under the runners. There was a magnificent sunset, and the snowy hills and deep blue water of the St. Lawrence Gulf seemed to rim in the splendour like a huge bowl of pearl and sapphire brimmed with wine and fire.

To the irrepressible Anne, winter is simply another season to experience fully and joyously.

Winter could be a merry time for Maud Montgomery as well, as when she recounts near-mishaps with the sleigh—getting stuck, tipping over, or, as during one storm when she was living in Belmont, becoming so lost that no one in her party knew where they were and her three male companions took to arguing about what to do next.

Finally, as the squall continued as thick as ever, we decided to take the wind in our faces and start. *If* the wind had not changed—a rather momentous "if"—this would take us across to Cape Malpeque. *If* it had—well, we might drive straight into the channel. In no very long

215

A winter sunset over the ice-covered Naufrage River.

time, however we reached land . . . There was no use in looking for a road—we just had to make one. We turned slap up the bank, tore a gap in a fence and drove across two fields . . . I expected every moment to hear the runners go smash.

The horses were terrified, the traces broke, and though "half frozen and wholly frightened," she also "shook with laughter" at the absurdity of the arguing boys. At last they reached the light for which they'd been aiming—a house "not half a mile from where we started."

This sense of humor was often the only way to cope with the season's brutal weather. "We have had a terrible two days' storm," she writes in 1905, the year she begins working in earnest on *Anne of Green Gables*. "I would say the worst storm we ever had if I didn't know that every bad storm seems the worst by reason of the contrast its present badness offers to the badness of past ones grown dim." The sequence of storms that winter and the amount of snow each delivered eventually created drifts as tall as the house, covering the doors and windows and leaving the rooms downstairs, "as dark as twilight. The drifts are certainly very beautiful; but one does not care greatly for architectural beauty in a prison." A week later she describes her pleasure at not having to "sally out and shovel snow . . . for the excellent reason that I could not get out. This morning the door and every window on the east side of the house was completely snowed over."

Some days, however, neither humor nor her writing could help her shake the weight or the length of the long nights (sixteen hours of darkness on the shortest day of the year); the effect on her was that of being imprisoned, with no escape from the depression that too often settled in during this time of year. "Winter is here to stay," she writes on the solstice in 1900.

Winter on the island means long, dark nights and the possibility of back-to-back snowstorms.

I hate it because I can't prowl around by myself outside in the evenings. When the dim wintry twilight comes down there is nothing to do but drop my work with a little sigh of weariness and creep away into a dark corner to nurse a bit of a heartache. If it were summer I could get away outside under the trees and the stars and my soul would be so filled with their beauty that pain would have no place.

Many of Maud's journal entries in winter read like the account of someone struggling with seasonal affective disorder. If she could just get outside; if she could just get enough sun! After a particularly fierce March storm left her with a case of "the blues," she writes, "I'll be all right when the sunshine comes back and I'm able to work." She finds some pleasure in forcing bulbs inside—daffodils, hyacinth, narcissus—their blossoms providing

219

Maud Montgomery's photograph of Lover's Lane on a day when she was able to get outside with her camera, despite the weather, c. 1890s. "I am no longer a prisoner," Montgomery wrote in her journal on March 11, 1904. "I can get out to the dear comradeship of woods and fields again. I went across the snowy fields to Lover's Lane. I love that place idolatrously—I am happier there than anywhere else."

ABOVE Horse and sleigh in winter, Prince Edward Island, c. 1860.

RIGHT A winter scene of the Cavendish home where Maud Montgomery lived with her grandparents. Photograph by L. M. Montgomery, c. 1890s.

a bit of color in the dead of winter. "I have some ... poking their dear heads up in window boxes and I have great hopes of them by and by." A few years later she writes of the effect of her daffodils, their beauty making her "feel ashamed of my blues and my despondency."

And even when the sun isn't shining, she can usually find in her work the necessary uplift that helps her transform the

221

Covehead Lighthouse in the winter, to the east of Cavendish Beach.

difficult into the beautiful. On one bitter night, when she's riding back from Charlottetown by sleigh after finishing her entrance exams, she writes that she "began to suffer keenly" from the chill. But after a stop to warm up, they set out again.

And I could once more enjoy the cold pure beauty of the landscape . . . The snow crackled and snapped under the runners. The sky faded out but the strip of yellow along the west got brighter and fierier, as if all the stray gleams of light were concentrating in one spot, and the long running curves of the distant hills stood out against it in dark distinctness and bare birches hung their slender boughs against the cold with the very perfection of grace.

222

Looking down from the highest cliff on the island at the Cape Tryon Lighthouse, just east of Park Corner.

It's just such exquisite moments that she carries over to *Anne of Green Gables*, giving Anne the same fierce energy of the season. When Anne bolts out the door to reunite with Diana after Minnie May's recovery—"gone without a cap or wrap . . . tearing through the orchard with her hair streaming"—Marilla tries calling out to her, "Anne Shirley—are you crazy? Come back this instant and put something on you." But of course it's too late, as Marilla quickly realizes, "I might as well call to the wind."

223

I had . . . then,
as now, two
great refuges and
consolations—the
world of nature and
the world of books.
They kept life in my
soul; they made me
love my home because
of my dreams and
rambles and the deep
joy and delight they
gave me—because
of the halo they
threw over what was
otherwise bare and
savorless.

—THE SELECTED JOURNALS OF
L. M. MONTGOMERY, VOL. 1

THAT GREAT AND SOLEMN WOOD

A WRITER'S LIFE

Maud Montgomery knew, even as a young girl, that no path other than becoming a writer could satisfy her desire to express what her imagination generated. While the forms of that work would not be clear for another decade, it became evident early on that her efforts would be intimately tied to the landscape in which she lived. She began keeping journals when she was eight (eventually destroying the earliest ones) and later copied and revised those she kept from age fourteen on, knowing that, with her increasing fame, even the details of her youth would be sought out by the public someday. The stakes thus became higher than simply using her journal to record and make meaning of events around her. She used her entries to cultivate a way of being in the world, enacting what she valued about the crafting of good literature—the honing of precise, original writing and of the narrative techniques involved in telling a good story.

227

A bookshelf at Green Gables, containing early primers (including *Latin Prose Composition*) and a fan that might have been needed on a warm day at church or at a concert.

She had learned the importance of a well-told tale or recitation early in her childhood, having come from a family that prided itself on its literary tastes, its level of education, and its many gifted storytellers; she even had a great uncle (Cousin Jimmie Macneill), who composed and recited hundreds of his own poems, none of which he ever wrote down.

She also immersed herself in the poetry available to her as a child—"Longfellow, Tennyson, Whittier, Scott, Byron, Milton, Burns," she writes in *The Alpine Path*—and could recite many of their poems from memory; they, in turn, helped shaped the beauty of her own writing and its lyrical evocation of the natural world. "Poetry pored over in childhood," she writes, "becomes part of one's nature more thoroughly than that which if first read in mature years can ever do. Its music was woven into my growing soul and has echoed through it, consciously and subconsciously, ever since."

Likewise, many of her characters are notable for their interest in literature and their ability to craft good stories—Anne Shirley tended to drive Marilla to distraction with her dramatic recounting of events real and imagined (unlike Matthew, who loved a good Anne story), and she even starts a story club so she and her friends can cultivate their fiction-writing skills. The protagonist of *The Story Girl* (whom Montgomery modeled on herself) is the central force of the novel through her eclectic and seemingly endless store of tales, and Captain Jim, of *Anne's House*

229

of Dreams, enlivens every gathering he attends with his extraordinary renderings of past experiences.

However, it's in *Emily of New Moon* that Montgomery reveals how the need to write and write well—particularly about the natural world—can define a life. For Emily, the character with whom Montgomery most identified, writing and "the flash" were intimately connected. "The flash," which "couldn't be described," characterized a moment when Emily found herself

> Very, very near to a world of wonderful beauty. Between it and herself hung only a thin curtain; she could never draw the curtain aside—but sometimes, just for a moment, a wind fluttered it and then it was as if she caught a glimpse of the enchanting realm beyond—only a glimpse—and heard a note of unearthly music.

That brief glimpse of the beyond propelled her to write. In one passage, she sees a mesmerizing scene, "the evening . . . bathed in a wonderful silence—and there was a sudden rift in the curdled clouds westward, and a lovely, pale, pinky-green lake of sky with a new moon in it," and she knows it would "hurt her with its beauty until she wrote it down."

Of course, for this sensitive, high-strung girl, writing is also a way to get revenge on her mean-spirited relatives and take the sting out of their insults. But more often the focus for Emily is to capture on paper that essence of beauty. To do it justice, the word choices had to be exactly right, along with the rhythm of each sentence. Even when she didn't have paper and pen, she soon found she could write in her head, which might make her late for a meal and her Aunt Elizabeth cross, but if she had found just the right sentence, little else seemed to matter.

Maud Montgomery believed *Emily of New Moon* (1923) to be "the best book I have ever written." She had made the same declaration after finishing *The Story Girl* in 1911 ("my own favourite

To a child with a lively imagination, any beautiful, wild thing could become much more—a flower to be woven into a garland, a place where fairies had gathered at night, a sight so stunning that she would have to labor to find the right words to describe it.

among my books," she wrote in *The Alpine Path*, "the one that gave me the greatest pleasure to write, the one whose characters and landscape seem to me most real"), and again after *Anne's House of Dreams* (1917). But five years later, *Emily* takes precedence: "I have had more intense pleasure in writing it than any of the others—not even excepting *Green Gables*. I have *lived* it, and I hated to pen the last line and write *finis*." This connection with Emily, and her ability to catch a glimpse of ideal beauty on the other side of a curtain, appears first in Montgomery's journal in 1905. "It has always seemed to me, ever since I can remember, that, amid all the commonplaces of life, I was very near to a kingdom of ideal beauty." A thin veil separates her from it, just as the curtain does in the novel, but when the wind causes it to flutter, there's a glimpse of what lies beyond, and "those glimpses have always made life worthwhile."

She repeats this again, modified only slightly, in *The Alpine Path*, suggesting that twelve years after the 1905 journal entry, she was still acutely aware of the fact that she could approximate beauty in her life and her work, having first found its form in the

231

Maud Montgomery, age twenty-two, Cavendish.

I cannot remember the
time when I was not
writing, or when I did not
mean to be an author.
—THE ALPINE PATH

Prince Edward Island landscapes—"the most beautiful place in [North] America, I believe"—but that the ideal lay just beyond, creating the kind of difficult and necessary goal that any serious artist strives to attain.

Despite its many pleasures, writing was also a tough pursuit, a "long, monotonous struggle," writes Montgomery in *The Alpine Path*, "a hard and steep path." Yet she chose to continue along it—perhaps channeling the advice of Anne Shirley's beloved teacher, Miss Stacy, that "I could learn to write well," as Anne relates it to Marilla, "if I only trained myself to be my own severest critic." For Montgomery that meant submitting work for publication, beginning when she was still in her teens. In those early years, rejections arrived far more often than acceptances, and even when a piece was published (the earliest appeared in print when she was sixteen and still living with her father in Saskatchewan), a check rarely followed. The first real money didn't arrive until 1895, when she was taking courses at Dalhousie College in Halifax, Nova Scotia, and a total of three checks appeared in one week: $5 for a letter written in verse; $12 for a poem; and $5 for a story, which sent her immediately into town to buy "five volumes of poetry . . . something I could keep for ever in memory of having 'arrived.'"

Heartened by this sense of arrival, she picked up her pace of writing and submitting, and the next several years brought

233

Though Maud Montgomery couldn't see the beach from the room where she worked in Cavendish, she knew by heart the way the sea wore away the red cliffs.

increasing success, with a growing list of publications, mostly for the Sunday school and children's/young adult market. As she writes in *The Alpine Path*:

> I have grubbed away industriously all this summer, and ground out stories and verses on days so hot that I feared my very marrow would melt and my gray matter be hopelessly sizzled up. But oh, I love my work! I love spinning stories, and I love to sit by the window of my room and shape some 'airy fairy' fancy into verse.

234

Bayberry and yarrow, a common pairing of plants near the Prince Edward Island shore in summer.

Not only did her early years ground her in the landscape and literature that she would rely on for the rest of her life, they also helped her establish a sense of discipline, a dogged determination to generate work for publication, despite circumstances over which she often had little control. Such fortitude was especially necessary during the year she spent teaching in Belmont. She was boarding with a family in a house that was always cold, working long hours to meet the needs of her students, and struggling to keep herself healthy ("I seem to have constant colds—the result of doing two teachers' work all winter and being half frozen most of the time"). She held fast to a daily schedule, waking early

235

A bedroom at Silver Bush. "From my earliest recollection," Montgomery wrote in her journal on March 2, 1901, "a visit to Silver Bush was the greatest treat in the world."

OPPOSITE The pond at Silver Bush was always a restorative place for the author.

to write before the fires were stoked, the family members had risen, and the school had to be opened. "I am sitting here half frozen," she notes in her journal, "for another cold snap is on and the mercury is down to 20 degrees below zero [C; minus 4 degrees F]. I have just finished my hour's writing at my new story and my fingers are so cold and cramped I can hardly hold the pen."

She would cite this experience again in *The Alpine Path* as a way to remind people who admired her literary gifts that serious writing required an equally serious practice. "I am inclined to wonder, with some inward amusement, how much they would have envied me on those dark, cold, winter mornings of my apprenticeship." For five months, she writes, "I got up at six o'clock and dressed by lamplight . . . I would put on a heavy coat and sit on my feet to keep them from freezing." And yet how she could transcend the frigid setting. "Sometimes it would be a poem in which I could carol blithely of blue skies and rippling brooks and flowery meads! Then I would thaw out my hands, eat breakfast and go to school."

237

References to this steady practice—the necessary daily ritual, the required focus, the wall she had to erect, at least temporarily, between herself and her immediate surroundings—appears often in her journals. "I have been writing as steadily as possible under rather uninspiring conditions," she writes in 1898, having moved back to Cavendish to care for her grandmother after her grandfather's death.

> How I love my work. I seem to grow more and more wrapped up in it as the days pass and other hopes and interests fail me. Nearly everything I think or do or say is subordinated to a desire to improve in my work. I study people and events for that, I think and speculate and read for that.

This dedication to writing was further honed in 1901 after a friend recommended her for a temporary job with a newspaper in Halifax, working as a copyeditor for the *Daily Echo*. The hum of office activity, the need to meet immediate deadlines, and the push to write about topics she wouldn't ordinarily have pursued, helped fine-tune her practice, though it seemed to surprise her when she discovered that she could block out all the newsroom noise and chaos and make time for her own work during lulls in the demands on her. The net result was that she earned more money from her own writing during this period than she did as an employee of the *Daily Echo*.

But seven months later she was back in Cavendish, again caring for her grandmother and confronting her prospects for the years ahead. In his will, her grandfather had bequeathed his property to his son but left no provision for the lifetime tenancy of his wife, and Uncle John F. Macneill was impatient to take possession, as his son, Preston, wanted to marry and needed a house. The resulting tensions made everyone miserable, Maud's grandmother, especially, who was stung by the treatment and insisted

Maud Montgomery, age thirty-four, the year *Anne of Green Gables* was published.

that she didn't want to be farmed out to another relative. Fortunately, Maud's very presence made ousting her grandmother unwarranted, while Maud's willingness to provide the necessary care and companionship made her uncle's demands seem even more cruel; the resulting bitterness between the four of them lasted the rest of their lives.

However, the future had become clearer: Maud knew that she would have to find her own living arrangement as soon as her grandmother died and that it was by her pen alone that she would achieve any financial security. At the time, many things were going well for her; she had a garden, she was making new friends, she was continuing to find success with stories and poems, and she had just met Ewan Macdonald, the new Presbyterian minister in Cavendish. Too, she had the idea for a novel about a girl orphan, who was sent to a couple wanting a boy, which she quietly kept to herself, along with the drive to see it to completion. Though she knew she had the talent to create such a book, nothing quite prepared her for the instant success of *Anne of Green Gables*.

Perhaps equally surprising was the effect that ongoing emotional turmoil wreaked on her, a sharp contrast to the optimistic personae that she and her sturdy girl characters—Anne Shirley, the Story Girl, Emily of New Moon, Pat of Silver Bush—presented to the world. It's in her journals that Montgomery reveals her struggles with despair, including a frightening period of "nervous prostration" that she suffered in 1910, the first of many debilitating episodes that would make daily life almost unbearable. "'That

241

which I feared' has come upon me," she wrote, "an utter break-down of body, soul, and spirit."

She had been cycling in and out of depression through-out the previous two years, feeling trapped by her grandmother's demands and seemingly petty rules for the house (no guests, no burning of extra lamps at night, no heating of the upstairs room during the winter). Her journal entries suggest that only an occasional walk outside, ideally along Lover's Lane, or the sight of bulbs in bloom on the sill—"a great comfort and sweetness to me"—could provide an antidote to the otherwise bleak winter months. As she wrote in December 1909:

> This evening, as I paced the floor in the twilight, listening to poor grandmother groaning with rheumatism, I smiled rather grimly as I contrasted my lot with what the world doubtless supposes it to be. I am a famous woman; I have written two very successful books. I have made a good bit of money. Yet, partly owing to Uncle John's behavior, partly to grandmother's immovable prejudices I can do nothing with my money to make life easier and more cheerful for grandmother and myself. And there is so much I might do if I could—fix up this old home comfortably, furnish it conveniently, keep a servant, travel a little, entertain my friends. But as it is I am as helpless as a chained prisoner.

It was an experience that would repeat itself for the rest of her life. Ironically, the patient Ewan Macdonald, who had agreed to postpone their marriage until after her grandmother died, was also prone to mental illness, which first showed up in their early courtship and became so severe later in life that he would require hospitalization. Often she worried as much about his emotional health as she did the effects of her own periods of despair.

In the years between such bouts, though, much about her life was rich and fulfilling, with all the rewards and challenges that

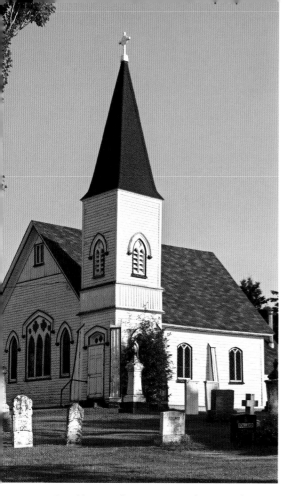

In addition to being a spiritual center of a community and the place to mark births, deaths, and marriages, churches also provided much social and cultural life.

Several denominations can be found in the larger communities; here, a Catholic church in Summerfield, Prince Edward Island.

came with being the mother of two children, the wife of a minister with an engaged congregation, and a world-famous author with all the professional and social obligations that accompanied such status. Throughout these years, her literary output remained prolific due in part to what her biographer, Mary Henley Rubio, describes as her "extraordinary ability to compartmentalize her life" and her choice to focus on things that nourished her. As Rubio writes:

> Maud took enormous pleasure in small things: seeing trilliums in the spring woods, growing flowers and vegetables in her summer garden, preparing desserts for church

243

socials, telling a story and making everyone laugh, looking at farmers harvesting crops, watching a winter sunset throw purple and mauve shadows over the snow, skimming over the rolling hills in a sleigh pulled by "Queen" (the Macdonalds' black mare), reading inside while a storm howled outside . . . It was Maud's basic nature to see the world as a luminous place, and she wrote glorious passages about it in her diary.

By 1914, she had to deal with another of the challenges on the writer's "hard and steep path," when she learned that L. C. Page, the Boston-based publisher who had first taken a chance on the author from Prince Edward Island, was selling reprint rights to her work without her permission and systematically cheating her on royalties. An increasingly bitter correspondence followed, as she tried to free herself from his punitive contracts and switch to a Canadian house, and he refused to negotiate or admit he owed her any payments; she eventually brought suit against him in 1918. Though she won the case and a settlement of $17,880, the victory was bittersweet, as, unbeknownst to her, he had sold the movie rights to *Anne of Green Gables* for $40,000. She was not to receive a penny from the 1919 silent film, nor from a second movie made in 1934.

In 1920, after his unauthorized publication of *Further Chronicles of Avonlea*, she was forced to sue him again, a costly litigation that dragged on for four years and necessitated several trips to Boston for long days in court. (She would ultimately have to file five separate lawsuits against him.) The experience exhausted her, dulling much of the shine from having secured a book publisher at age thirty-two, when she was the assistant postmistress of a tiny island town, living under her grandmother's roof.

Ultimately, the joy and respite she found in writing, whether crafting lengthy journal entries or plotting out a new novel, weren't enough to keep her from the approach of another

Maud Montgomery, age sixty-one, Norval, Ontario.

Daylilies alongside Silver Bush.

bout of depression. Ewan's mental illness, the pending horror of another world war, and the challenges and disappointments associated with her older son, Chester, had taken too great a toll. In a letter written in 1941, urging a nephew not to enlist (a copy of which is framed on the wall at Silver Bush), she lists some of the other worries she bears:

> Chester's wife has left him and gone home to her father . . . He has broken our hearts this past 10 years . . . My heart is broken and it is that has broken me. I have to have a nurse and can't afford it. I am not and never [was] the rich woman I was supposed to be . . . I can hardly write—my nerves are so terrible . . . I think my mind is going. Rest from worry is what I need and I cannot get that anywhere. I am alone.

Another document, found next to her body after she overdosed on drugs the following spring, was numbered so as to appear as the last page of her journal.

> I have lost my mind by spells and I do not dare to think what I may do in those spells. May God forgive me and I hope everyone else will forgive me even if they cannot understand. My position is too awful to endure and nobody realizes it. What an end to a life in which I tried always to do my best in spite of many mistakes.

In the end, Maud Montgomery was unable to return to the sense of fulfillment described in the final sentences of *The Alpine Path*: "It was not an easy ascent, but even in the struggle at its hardest there was a delight and a zest known only to those who aspire to the heights." Lines from Keats had inspired her—"He ne'er is crowned / With immortality, who fears to follow / Where airy voices lead"—to which she wholeheartedly agreed.

247

The cemetery in Cavendish, where visitors enter under a tall archway bearing the inscription "Resting Place of L. M. Montgomery."

True, most true! We must follow our "airy voices," follow them through bitter suffering and discouragement and darkness, through doubt and disbelief, through valleys of humiliation and over delectable hills where sweet things would lure us from our quest, ever and always must we follow, if we would reach the "far-off divine event" and look out thence to the aerial spires of our City of Fulfilment.

Until her journals were published, few knew of Montgomery's struggles to reconcile her inner despair with the optimism she sought to project to the people around her. As Mary Henley Rubio writes, to the outside world Montgomery was "a successful author, a dynamo in her community, a powerful speaker in public, a performer for charitable causes, a woman whose intellectual range made her a fascinating conversationalist in social gatherings, and a warm and likeable human being with a very fine sense of humor." To readers of her novels, she was the creator of resourceful, fiercely imaginative characters, who were well equipped to deal with life's challenges, and knew how to tap the life force in the natural world around them when the going got tough.

We can only wonder whether her health would have improved had she found a way to return to the landscapes of Prince Edward Island, to the delectable hills and airy spires she immortalized in *Anne of Green Gables*. As her writings insist, those

249

are the places that gave her and her characters their strength. Even in winter, often the grimmest of seasons, the natural world of the island had supplied her with moments of profound peace, which she does not write about finding anywhere else. "I feel a wonderful lightness of spirit," she writes, when outside on a moonlit winter night, "and a soul-stirring joy in mere existence . . . a joy that seems to spring fountain-like from the very deeps of my being and to be independent of all earthy things."

 Such moments come rarely . . . but when they do come they are inexpressibly marvelous and beautiful . . . as if the finite were for a second infinity . . . as if humanity were for a space uplifted into divinity. Only for a moment, 'tis true . . . yet such a moment is worth a cycle of common years untouched by the glory and the dream.

The ellipses, which appear in the original, seem to mark those singular times when, moved by the exquisite scene in the landscape that surrounds her, she has caught a glimpse of the curtain between her and ideal beauty. She pauses the sentence and waits—the wind blows, the curtain flutters, the vision comes into focus again—and on she goes, putting more words on the page, finding new ways to bridge the worlds of nature and spirit, moving ever closer to inhabiting the place where humanity is at last "uplifted into divinity."

A red road on Prince Edward Island, with its open
invitation to wander and wonder.

Autumn colors on Prince Edward Island.

RESOURCES

In addition to the primary destination for visitors to Prince Edward Island—the Green Gables Heritage Place in Cavendish—the following resources, both real and virtual, provide greater context for the life and times of Maud Montgomery and Anne Shirley.

Anne of Green Gables Museum
4542 Route 20, Park Corner, PE, Canada
annemuseum.com

The house at Park Corner (home to her dear relatives, Aunt Annie and Uncle John Campbell), which Montgomery called Silver Bush, is where she spent some of the happiest times of her early life and found inspiration for many of her stories. Still owned by the Campbell family, the property has become an important museum for readers interested in knowing more about Montgomery and the characters in her novels. In addition to a tour of the house, which includes the parlor where Maud Montgomery married Ewan Macdonald, visitors can walk alongside the Lake of Shining Waters, take a carriage ride with a Matthew Cuthbert look-alike, or wander through the adjacent apple orchard.

Avonlea Village

8779 Route 6, Cavendish, PE, Canada

avonlea.ca

A half mile east of Green Gables, Avonlea Village offers visitors a chance to see original buildings from Montgomery's time. The schoolhouse where she taught in Belmont and the Long River parsonage and church that she attended with her family were moved to the site and carefully restored, while replicas of other period buildings were added to create a sense of a small community. For many years, visitors were treated to scenes of craftspeople engaged with the activities of Anne's time; the emphasis now is on shops and restaurants, and the site often hosts weddings and other Anne-influenced celebrations.

Canada's Historic Places

www.gov.pe.ca/hpo/index.php3?number=1022313&lang=E

This website identifies houses of significance to L.M. Montgomery that are included on both the Prince Edward Island and the Canada registers of historic places. Locations appear in the order in which Montgomery became associated with them, with architectural information about each along with relevant quotations from Montgomery's writings.

The Confederation Centre of the Arts

145 Richmond Street, Charlottetown, PE, Canada

confederationcentre.com/en/index.php

The Confederation Centre Art Gallery houses Montgomery's two earliest scrapbooks (covering the period from 1893 to 1909) during the winter; they spend the rest of the year at her birthplace in New London, where they're protected under glass. A virtual exhibit of Montgomery's scrapbooks can be seen at: http://lmm. confederationcentre.com/english/scrapbooks/scrapbooks.html#.

Green Gables Heritage Place

8619 Cavendish Road, Cavendish, PE, Canada

pc.gc.ca/en/lhn-nhs/pe/greengables

The green-gabled farmhouse that became L. M. Montgomery's inspiration for the home Anne Shirley would share with the Cuthberts is now a National Historic Site managed by Canada's national park service, Parks Canada. Visitors can tour the house, with its period furnishings and rooms that evoke the fictional characters, and explore the grounds, including Lover's Lane, Balsam Hollow and the Haunted Wood.

The Leaskdale Manse

11850 Durham Regional Road 1, Leaskdale, ON, Canada

lucymaudmontgomery.ca

The first home Montgomery could call her own, and where she designed her first garden, is a National Historic Site, along with the adjacent church where Ewan was minister; both are open to the public.

The L. M. Montgomery Birthplace

6461 Route 20 (at the intersection with Route 6), New London, PE, Canada

Designated as a historic site due to its architectural integrity, this small frame house, relatively unchanged since Maud Montgomery's birth in 1874, is now a museum, where guides offer informative tours of rooms outfitted in period furniture. Here visitors can see the room where Montgomery was born, a replica of the dress and shoes she wore at her wedding, as well as scrapbooks she maintained.

The L. M. Montgomery Literary Society

http://lmmontgomeryliterarysociety.weebly.com/
Based in the Midwest, the L. M. Montgomery Literary Society is a resource for enthusiasts all over the world. The website includes a chronology with links for creating a self-guided literary tour of Montgomery-associated sites, both on PEI and in Ontario, as well as information for collectors of L. M. Montgomery's books.

The Lucy Maud Montgomery Heritage Garden

477 Guelph Street, Norval, ON, Canada
gardenofthesenses.com
In Norval, volunteers helped create the Lucy Maud Montgomery Heritage Garden at her home with a "Garden of the Senses" designed as an interactive engagement with the same species of plants found in *Anne of Green Gables.*

Macphail Woods Ecological Forestry Project

269 Macphail Park Road., Orwell, PE, Canada
macphailwoods.org
For visitors interested in the restoration of native forests, Macphail Woods (a twenty-minute drive east of Charlottetown) is a research facility that offers walking trails, an arboretum, and a native plant nursery. The nature guides available on the website offer information and photographs of local flora and fauna. Additional Prince Edward Island walking trails can be found at islandtrails.ca/en/index.php; the trail closest to Green Gables, the Breadalbane Natural Trail, follows the Dunk River through stands of spruce trees and mixed hardwoods, with long stretches

257

of ferns and woodland blossoms that evoke Anne Shirley's childhood.

The Site of L. M. Montgomery's Cavendish Home: The Macneill Homestead

Route 6, a quarter-mile east of Green Gables Heritage Place, Cavendish
lmmontgomerycavendishhome.com

The site of the house Montgomery shared with her grandparents and where she wrote *Anne of Green Gables*, as well as hundreds of other stories and poems, offers visitors a sense of the old homestead. The foundation site remains, surrounded by old apple trees, with a vegetable and flower garden nearby. Staff at the small museum and bookstore can provide excellent background information on Maud's life and times. A trail from the homesite crosses Route 6 and winds through the Haunted Wood to Green Gables.

The University of Guelph Library

50 Stone Road East, Guelph, ON, Canada
lmmrc.ca

For those interested in learning more about Maud Montgomery, the L. M. Montgomery Research Centre website is an invaluable resource. Hundreds of historic photos, many taken by Maud Montgomery, along with pages from her early journals and scrapbooks have been scanned and cataloged and can now be viewed digitally, while more material from the archive continues to be added on a regular basis.

A wash stand at Green Gables.

NOTES

All of the quoted material in the book, unless otherwise noted, is from L. M. Montgomery. Whenever possible, her writings were used to capture the essence of the landscapes of Prince Edward Island. She—and by extension, Anne Shirley—knew the island's natural world so intimately that any attempt to paraphrase her work would diminish its elegance and risk missing the nuances of light and shadow, color and season, and time of day or night she knew so well. For both "Lucy Maud," as the islanders call her, and Anne of Green Gables, the beauty of Prince Edward Island is intricately linked to the workings of their imaginations; by spending time with Montgomery's descriptions, we can begin to see how such a place could shape one's very character and, in turn, make Prince Edward Island such a memorable landscape to a worldwide audience of appreciative readers.

Source abbreviations

AGG   L. M. Montgomery, *Anne of Green Gables.* Boston: L. C. Page and Company, 1908. Norton Critical Edition edited by Mary Henley Rubio and Elizabeth Waterston. NY: Norton, 2007.

AHD   L. M. Montgomery, *Anne's House of Dreams.* Toronto: McClelland, Goodchild, and Stewart; New York: Frederick A. Stokes Company, 1917.

AP   L. M. Montgomery, *The Alpine Path: The Story of My Career.* Don Mills, Ontario: Fitzhenry & Whiteside, Ltd, 1917.

AV   L. M. Montgomery, *Anne of Avonlea.* Boston: L. C. Page and Company, 1909.

CM   *The Canadian Magazine*

ENM   L. M. Montgomery, *Emily of New Moon.* Toronto: McClelland and Stewart; New York: Frederick A. Stokes Company, 1923.

LMM   Mary Henley Rubio, *Lucy Maud Montgomery: The Gift of Wings*. Toronto: Anchor Canada, 2008.

SJ   L. M. Montgomery, *The Selected Journals of L. M. Montgomery*, vols. 1–3. Edited by Mary Rubio and Elizabeth Waterston. Ontario: Oxford University Press, 1985–1992.

SP   Francis W. L. Bolger, *Spirit of Place: Lucy Maud Montgomery and Prince Edward Island*. NY: Oxford University Press, 1983.

Citations to sources

Page

7. These lines from Robert Browning's poem "Evelyn Hope" appear as the epigraph to *AGG*. The wording of the second line deviates slightly from the original poem, which reads: "The good stars met in your horoscope / Made you of spirit, fire and dew."

This Island Is the Bloomiest Place: An Introduction

17. "we fairly lived": *SJ*, vol. 1, Aug. 15, 1892, 83.

Kindred Orphans: The Lives of Maud Montgomery and Anne Shirley

23. "I would like": *SJ*, vol. 1, July 26, 1896, 162.

28. "I put my arm": *SJ*, vol. 1, Mar. 6, 1892, 78.

28. "I have *never* drawn": *SJ*, vol. 2, Jan. 27, 1911, 38.

29. "When I am asked": *SJ*, vol. 2, Jan. 27, 1911, 39–40.

31. "a real mother": *SJ*, vol. 1, Jan. 7, 1910, 383.

31. "It gave me exquisite": *SJ*, vol. 1, Jan. 7, 1910, 383.

35. "My childish faults" and "I resented this": *SJ*, vol. 1, Jan. 2, 1905, 301.

35. "lover of nature" and "a rich, poetic": *SJ*, vol. 1, Jan. 7, 1910, 382.

35. "stern, domineering": *SJ*, vol. 1, Jan. 2, 1905, 301.

35. "He bruised my": *SJ*, vol. 1, Jan. 2, 1905, 301.

35. "It's terrible lonesome": *AGG*.

36. "kind . . . in a": *SJ*, vol. 1, Jan. 2, 1905, 301.

36. "I was constantly": *SJ*, vol. 1, Jan. 2, 1905, 301.

36. "Emotionally they grew": *SJ*, vol. 1, Jan. 2, 1905, 302.

37. "I was impulsive": *SJ*, vol. 1, Jan. 2, 1905, 301.

39. "I *cannot* call": *SJ*, vol. 1, Oct. 6, 1890, 33.

41. "reads all my" and "is so cross": *SJ*, vol. 1, Oct. 6, 1890, 33.

41. "The truth of": *SJ*, vol. 1, July 21, 1891, 57.

41. "that he finds": *SJ*, vol. 1, Aug. 26, 1890, 30.

41. "Father is a poor": *SJ*, vol. 1, May 14, 1891, 50.

42. "Oh, for one glimpse": *SJ*, vol. 1, Aug. 20, 1890, 29.

42. "Of course I know": *SJ*, vol. 1, Dec. 11, 1890, 37.

44. "pink and white": *SJ*, vol. 1, May 13, 1890, 20.

44. "I long for the sight": *SJ*, vol. 1, April 25, 1897, 185.

45. "must be the souls": *AGG*.

47. "I always say good": *AGG*.

47. "talking in their" and "dreams they must": *AGG*.

47. "made friends" and "been lonesome": *AGG*.

47. "I just love": *SJ*, vol. 1, Oct. 11, 1889, 3.

47. "In the woods": letter to G. B. MacMillan, Sept. 16, 1906; quoted in *SP*.

47. "Anne's habit": *SJ*, vol. 2, Jan. 27, 1911, 40.

50. "was of course": *SJ*, vol. 2, Jan. 27, 1911, 42.

50. "the effects of": *SJ*, vol. 2, Jan. 27, 1911, 40.

51. "As far back": *SJ*, vol. 2, Jan. 27, 1911, 41.

52. "If I really": *AGG*.

52. "I have an ideal": *SJ*, vol. 1, July 26, 1896, 162.

55. "tattered, beclayed," "faces plastered," and "We were picking": *SJ*, vol. 1, Sept. 25, 1899, 2.

55. "It has been" and "It just seemed": *SJ*, vol. 1, Oct. 20, 1890, 34.

57–58. "entirely too much," "more and more," and "while this odd": *AGG*.

The Loveliest Spot on Earth: Prince Edward Island Then and Now

70. "Mr. Bell having": *AGG*.

79. "always rustling": *AGG*.

82. "I consider it": *SJ*, vol. 1, Apr. 12, 1903, 287.

82. "I love this": *SJ*, vol. 1, Mar. 16, 1904, 294.

85. "idolatrously" and "happier there": *SJ*, vol. 1, Mar. 11, 1904, 292.

85. "It is the dearest" and "and has the greatest": *SJ*, vol. 1, Oct. 8, 1899, 243.

86. "through so many": *AGG*.

89. "shimmering and blue": *AGG*.

96. "the last happy" and "whole past life": *SJ*, vol. 1, Jan. 7, 1910, 390.

100. "the hardest I": *SJ*, vol. 1, Jan. 7, 1910, 391.

100. "no leafy lanes": *SJ*, vol. 1, April 25, 1897, 185.

101. "A year of": *SJ*, vol. 1, Jan. 7, 1910, 391.

103. "It is evening": *SJ*, vol. 1, May 1, 1899, 238.

Something More Poetical: The Scope of Two Imaginations

108. "it would be" and "This island is": *AGG*.

110. "shone like a" and "queer funny ache": *AGG*.

110. "Oh, isn't it," "small and wormy," and "Oh, I don't": *AGG*.

112. "it was really": *AGG*.

112. "could have found": *AGG*.

112–113. "I was firmly" and "I was trying": *AGG*.

113. "gorgeous dreamland": *AGG*.

113. "Isn't it fortunate": *AGG*.

113, 116. "for goodness sake," "receive the lily," and "Anne looked at": *AGG*.

116. "Will you ever" and "Don't give up": *AGG*.

118. "I was so": *AP*.

118. "Oh, we have": *AGG*.

118. "preferring to take" and "A white strip": *AGG*.

119. "The night was" and "truly delightful": *AGG*.

120. "Came dancing home": *AGG*.

121. "Grandfather doesn't": *SJ*, vol. 1, Dec. 23, 1895, 150.

121. "its roofs and spires," "tiny dark headlands," "baleful star," "a concave," and "with a maiden": *SJ*, vol. 1, Dec. 23, 1895, 150.

124. "a thunderbolt from": *SJ*, vol. 1, May 1, 1900, 248.

124. "Even when he": *SJ*, vol. 1, May 1, 1900, 249.

124, 126. "With the effort" and "Oh, as long": *SJ*, vol. 1, May 1, 1900, 249.

126. "It was lovely": *SJ*, vol. 1, Nov. 20, 1906, 324.

127. "one can dream," "so painfully bare," and "was of a": *AGG*.

128. "Marilla had eyed" and "it's the eatables": *AGG*.

129–132. "a couple of," "How I love," "a tree in some," "so utterly," and "It is hard": *SJ*, vol. 1, April 25, 1897, 185.

137–138. "red fields smoking" and "Marilla's sober": *AGG*.

143. "Every little cove": *AGG*.

Emerald Screens: Maud's and Anne's Favorite Gardens

145. "It is the greatest": *SJ*, vol. 1, July 30, 1905, 307.

148. "Fair, rich confusion": Anna Bartlett Warner quoted in May Brawley Hill, *Grandmother's Garden: The Old-Fashioned American Garden, 1865–1915*, NY: Abrams, 1995, 29.

151. "There is nothing": *SJ*, vol. 1, Aug. 28, 1901, 263–264.

155. "be born not": *SJ*, vol. 1, Aug. 28, 1901, 263.

156. "sweet old-fashioned": *AGG*.

157. "she did not like": *AV*.

159. "My garden—oh": *SJ*, vol. 1, July 30, 1905, 307.

161. "We have been:" *SJ*, vol. 2, May 18, 1913, 119.

161. "a perfect river": *SJ*, vol. 2, Sept. 1, 1919, 324.

162. "very old-fashioned": "A Garden of Old Delights," *CM,* June 1910.

165. "old Mrs. George": *SJ*, vol. 1, Aug. 28, 1901, 263.

173. "there is no sweeter": *AGG*.

173. "delicious aroma": *AV*.

173. "no soft blending" and "the only things": *AHD*.

174–175. "A Prince Edward" and "my favorite object": *SJ*, vol. 2, April 15, 1914, 145.

177. "All the little wood": *AGG*.

177. "a June dawn": *AHD*.

A World With Octobers: The Seasons of Prince Edward Island

183. "Spring is the best": "Spring in the Woods," *CM*, vol. 37, no. 1, May 1911, 59.

189. "the initials of": "Spring in the Woods," *CM*, vol. 37, no. 1, May 1911, 60.

189. "all the grass": "Spring in the Woods," *CM*, vol. 37, no. 1, May 1911, 60.

189. "those shyest": *AGG*.

189. "pale, aerial": *AGG*.

189. "Spring—spring": *SJ*, vol. 2, April 15, 1914, 145.

192. "Believe me": "Spring in the Woods," *CM*, vol. 37, no. 1, May 1911, 59.

195. "It was a girl": *AGG*.

196. "The spring woods": *CM*, vol. 37, no. 5, Sept. 1911, 399.

197. "Who that has": "The Woods in Summer," *CM*, vol. 37, no. 5, Sept. 1911, 399.

197. "the golden summer": *AGG*.

197. "dancing up the": *AGG*.

199. "Haying began today": *SJ*, vol. 1, July 24, 1899, 238.

201. "A cool wind": *AGG*.

202. "as big as our fists": *AP*.

207. "All the gaps": *AGG*.

208. "Isn't this evening": *AGG*.

208–211. "Harvest is ended" and "It is October": *SJ*, vol. 1, Oct. 7, 1897, 195.

211. "curled up Turk-fashion": *AGG*.

211. "the infinite sadness": *SJ*, vol. 1, Oct. 7, 1897, 195.

213. "people like to": *SJ*, vol. 1, Dec. 31, 1891, 71.

213. "in the wonderful": *AGG*.

215. "Anne revelled": *AGG*.

215–218. "Finally, as the"; "half frozen"; "shook with laughter"; "not half a mile": *SJ*, vol. 1, Jan. 27, 1897, 177–178.

218. "We have had" and "I would say"; *SJ*, vol. 1, Jan. 27, 1905, 303.

218. "as dark as"; *SJ*, vol. 1, Jan. 27, 1905, 303.

218. "sally out": *SJ*, vol. 1, Feb. 8, 1905, 303.

219. "I hate it": *SJ*, vol. 1, Dec. 22, 1900, 254.

219. "the blues" and "I'll be all": *SJ*, vol. 1, Mar. 16, 1904, 294.

221. "I have some": *SJ*, vol. 1, Dec. 10, 1905, 311.

221. "feel ashamed of": *SJ*, vol. 1, Jan. 20, 1907, 329.

222. "began to suffer" and "And I could": *SJ*, vol. 1, Dec. 22, 1893, 98–99.

That Great and Solemn Wood: A Writer's Life

225. "I had . . . then": *SJ*, vol. 1, Jan. 2, 1905, 301.

230. "the best book": *SJ*, vol. 3, Feb. 15, 1922, 39.

231. "I have had": *SJ*, vol. 3, Feb. 15, 1922, 39.

231. "It has always" and "those glimpses": *SJ*, vol. 1, Jan. 2, 1905, 301.

233. "I could learn" and "if I only": *AGG*.

233. "five volumes": *AP*.

235. "I seem to have": *SJ*, vol. 1, April 9, 1897, 183.

237. "I am sitting" and "for another cold": *SJ*, vol. 1, Mar. 1, 1897, 181.

238. "I have been writing" and "How I love my": *SJ*, vol. 1, Dec. 31, 1898, 228.

241. "I am so": *SJ*, vol. 1, May 24, 1908, 334.

241–242. "nervous prostration" and "'That which I feared'": *SJ*, vol. 1, Feb. 7, 1910, 392.

242. "a great comfort": *SJ*, vol. 1, Dec. 23, 1909, 362.

242. "This evening, as": *SJ*, vol. 1, Dec. 26, 1909, 364–365.

243–244. "Maud took enormous": *LMM*, 172.

247. "I have lost": quoted in *LMM*, 576.

249. "a successful author": *LMM*, 299.

250. "I feel a" and "Such moments come": "The Woods in Winter," *CM*, vol. 38, no. 2, Dec. 1911, 164.

ACKNOWLEDGMENTS

I am indebted to Drs. Mary Henley Rubio and Elizabeth Hillman Waterston for their scholarship and meticulous editing of Maud Montgomery's journals; the resulting five-volume set, *The Selected Journals of L. M. Montgomery*, helped me better understand the author's complicated heart and mind, her unwavering commitment to writing, and her deep love for the landscapes of Prince Edward Island.

I also send much appreciation to Nick Jay for his stunning photographs of Prince Edward Island through the seasons; to Evan Raskin, biologist extraordinaire with the National Park Service, who brought his expertise to bear at a critical juncture; to Mary Beth Cavert and Carolyn Strom Collins of the L. M. Montgomery Literary Society for their very helpful reviews; and to the Anne of Green Gables Licensing Authority, the heirs of L. M. Montgomery, and literary consultant Sally Keefe Cohen for their permission to work with this material. All those at Timber Press who had a hand on this project helped improve it, with the talented Mollie Firestone bringing the final pieces together with much tact and grace. If errors remain, they are my own.

Numerous others helped with various stages of this undertaking, and I offer sincere thanks to all of them: Debra Spark, who first sent the project my way, and Juree Sondker, for making it sound possible; Cindy Rice, long-time Prince Edward Island resident, for the visits that bookended my trips over the years, and for delaying the long cross-Canada drive so we could have a few more hours together; Joyce and Gil Johnson, who gave me a boost at an early stage with photos and books and memories from their decades of summers spent on the island; Betty MacPhee and Jennie Macneill, of L. M. Montgomery's Cavendish Home, who patiently answered so many of my questions; Paige Matthie, registrar at the Confederation Centre of the Arts in Charlottetown, Prince Edward Island, for assistance with accessing Maud Montgomery's scrapbooks; and Peter LoIacono, for Whispering Fields, his lovely, off-the-grid cabin in the heart of the island.

I thank, too, the many friends who shared their early memories of *Anne of Green Gables*, especially Rachel Haley Himmelheber, Sally Reid and the circle of friends she tapped, Hannah Poston, and Elizabeth Kostova.

Finally, heartfelt thanks go to Kerry Michaels, as much for her gorgeous photography as for the many messages (witty, timely) and additional images (always inspiring) that helped sustain me during the long writing time; to my dear brother and intrepid traveler, Douglas Reid, whose presence deeply enriched the days we shared on the island; and to Catherine Peck, whose friendship made all the difference during a long spring of transitions. Gratitude to you all.

The ever-changing Cavendish Beach.

PHOTO AND ILLUSTRATION CREDITS

Catherine Reid, page 82

Douglas H. Reid, page 86

Emily Weigel, pages 1, 10, 24, 62, 106, 146, 184, 226

Imagining Anne: The Island Scrapbooks of L. M. Montgomery, edited by Dr. Elizabeth Epperly, published in 2008, is published by Penguin Random House Inc., pages 136 left, 136 right, 137, 138

Kerry Michaels, pages 2, 8–9, 14, 15, 16, 18, 19, 22–23, 26–27, 30, 31, 39, 40, 46, 49, 53, 54, 57, 60–61, 64, 68, 69, 72, 73, 74 top left, 74 top right, 75, 76, 77 top, 77 bottom, 79, 80, 81, 83, 88, 89 left, 89 top right, 89 bottom right, 90, 92, 93 top, 93 bottom, 94, 95, 96, 98–99, 100, 101, 102–103, 104–105, 108, 109, 110 left, 110 right, 111, 112, 119 left, 119 right, 120, 122, 125, 127 left, 127 right, 128 left, 128 right, 130, 131, 132, 134, 139, 140 left, 140 right, 141, 142–143, 144–145, 148, 150, 152 left, 152 right, 153, 155, 158, 159 left, 159 right, 160, 164, 166, 168 left, 168 right, 169 left, 169 right, 170–171, 172–173, 174 left, 176 top left, 176 top right, 176 bottom right, 176 bottom left, 178, 179 right, 187, 190, 203 left, 203 right, 224–225, 228, 231, 234, 235, 236, 237, 240, 243 left, 243 right, 246, 248, 251, 259, 270

L. M. Montgomery Collection, Archival & Special Collections, University of Guelph Library, pages 20, 32, 33, 34 bottom, 34 top left, 34 top right, 35, 36, 37, 38, 48, 51, 56, 59, 78, 87, 91, 97, 135, 161, 162, 163, 165, 179 left, 181, 194, 198, 199, 200, 204, 220, 221 bottom, 232, 239, 245

Nicholas Jay, pages 6–7, 71, 182–183, 188–189, 191 left, 191 right, 192, 193, 195, 196, 201, 202, 205, 206–207, 208, 209, 210–211, 212–213, 214, 216–217, 219, 222, 223, 252–253

Public Archives and Records Office of PEI, Acc3466/ HF74.27.3.7, page 45

Public Archives and Records Office of PEI, Acc3466/ HF72.66.22.6, page 67

Public Archives and Records Office of PEI, Acc3466/ HF74.27.3.22, page 221 top

Sarah Burwash, endpapers

Special Collections, USDA National Agricultural Library

Unknown. 1897. "Miss C. H. Lippincott," page 156

Unknown. 1902. "Child's Rare Flowers, Vegetables, and Fruits," page 154 left

Unknown. 1902. "E. J. Bowen's Seed Stores, Seed Manual," page 157

Unknown. 1902. "Farquhar's Seeds," page 154 right

Wikimedia Commons

Used under an Attribution–ShareAlike 2.0 Generic license

Joshua Mayer, page 175 right

Ole Husby, page 174–175

Public domain

Paul Sherman of WPClipart, page 44

Illustrations by M. A. and W. A. J. Claus, from the 1908 edition of *Anne of Green Gables*, pages 13, 43, 84, 114, 115, 117, 280

INDEX

Webb, Ernest, 32
wheat, 18, 26, 187
"White Lady" (tree), 59
"the White Way of Delight", 108
Whittier, John Greenleaf, 155, 229
wild gardens, 147, 167–171
wild lily of the valley, 85, 175, 177
Willowmere, 50, 175, 193
willow sprays, 129
winter, 213–223
woodland gardens, 147, 173–180
woods, 47, 111, 140, 174

Y
yarrow, 235

"'COME, I'M GOING TO WALK HOME WITH YOU.'"

Illustration by M. A. and W. A. J. Claus, from the 1908 edition.

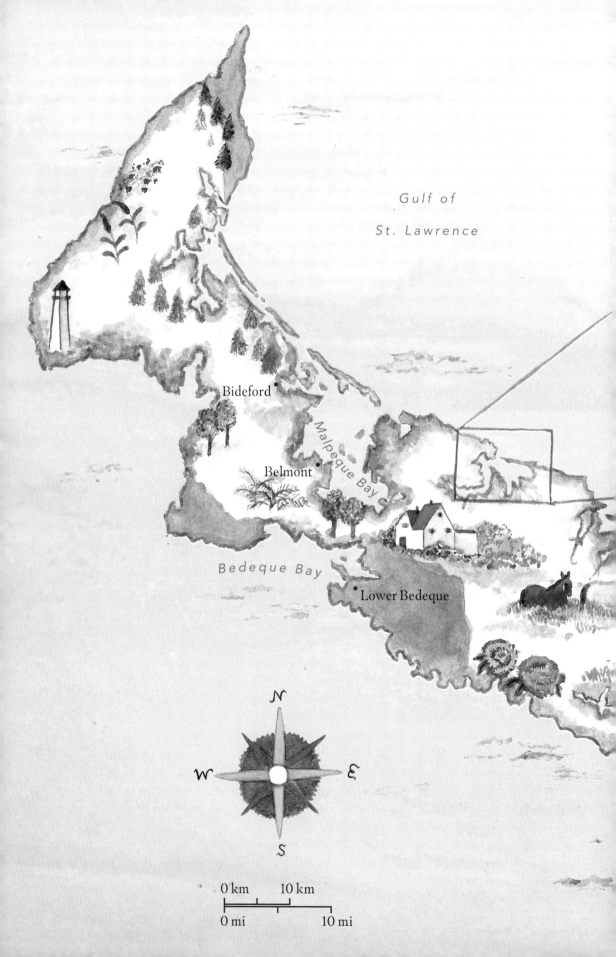

Gulf of

St. Lawrence

Bideford

Belmont

Malpeque Bay

Bedeque Bay

Lower Bedeque

N

W

E

S

0 km   10 km

0 mi   10 mi